The God's Country Naturalist

Outdoor Blessings

Kevin Starner

First Edition

ISBN 978-0-692-95159-0

Printed in the United States of America

To Leann, for tolerating my eccentricities, indulging my outdoor habits, and keeping me on the straight and narrow path.

You are worthy, our Lord and God, to receive glory and honor and power, for you created all things, and by your will they were created and have their being.

(Revelations 4:11)

Contents

Preface

Watching a big buck unknowingly approach your treestand, calling a strutting gobbler to within a few feet of your setup, catching a native brook trout on a well-placed dry fly, spotting a rare bird well outside its known range – these are just a few of the myriad blessings that an outdoorsman is likely to experience when spending time afield in God's natural creation.

Most Christian outdoorsmen would generally agree that God's natural creation and the time spent in it can be a source of great joy, inspiration, and fulfillment. Engaging in the physical acts of hunting, fishing, and bird watching requires the participant to be in direct contact with nature for the express purpose of accomplishing a perceived goal or objective (e.g., to get a deer, to catch a trout, etc.). While not always successful in these endeavors, the time spent outdoors enjoying the sights and sounds of God's natural creation is always a rewarding experience. When success does occur, the rewards, as one might expect, are even sweeter. Either way, God's blessings abound in nature, and lucky is the person who learns this firsthand.

Beyond these more surficial benefits, however, there exists a deeper, underlying spiritual truth that comes from spending time outdoors. This spiritual truth was embedded in the earth at the time of creation and has been calling to all those who are willing to listen since the dawn of time. The Apostle Paul wrote about this when he declared that God's invisible qualities – His eternal power and divine nature – can be clearly seen in the creative grandeur of the natural world (Romans 1:20). All one needs to do to understand this profound reality is to submit their life to

Christ, and then this underlying spiritual truth will be as plainly visible as if it was written in the clouds or carved on a mountain. When this happens, God's remarkable goodness will be manifested in all your outdoor activities, regardless of the outcome. Therein resides the impetus for the writing of this book.

Outdoor Blessings, the third and final installment in The God's Country Naturalist Series, is a collection of outdoor adventure stories that tries to capture some of the godly blessings that can only come from spending time afield hunting, fishing, and bird watching. These personal accounts are reflective of some of my most memorable experiences in the great outdoors, but they are more than just your standard hunting and fishing tales. Each one is a standalone testimony of Christian faith derived through introspective reflection on God's divine nature, or at least so much as I understand it from having spent the better part of my adult life observing, studying, and learning about His natural creation.

In sharing these various stories, I am hopeful that you will be inspired to pull on a pair of boots, grab your binoculars, and head outdoors to see what good things the Lord may have in store for you. In so doing, I am confident that God's natural creation and the time spent in it will prove to be a blessing to you too.

Kevin Starner

Adventures in Hunting

The Blessing Buck

God's blessings come in many shapes and forms for the deer hunter. The revealing glow of a cold November sunrise, a gentle breeze to blow the human scent away, the rich autumn aroma of freshly fallen leaves, and the peaceful solitude that comes from time spent in the woods are just a few examples of the godly blessings that a deer hunter is likely to experience.

Of course, none of these things are quite as tangible or as rewarding as harvesting a mature buck, which is the ultimate outdoor blessing that every deer hunter desires. It's the possibility of getting a big buck (however probable or improbable that may be) that drives many of us hunters to the woods each and every fall to see what the Good Lord has in store for us.

It's with this thought in mind that I reflect upon the happenings of the 2015 Archery Season. As an avid deer hunter, I was looking forward to the coming archery season with much enthusiasm and anticipation. However, as the waning days of summer finally gave way to fall, I found myself entangled in one of the worst schedule conflicts of my life. The combination of work, family, and civic responsibilities had escalated to the point of being unmanageable. I was being pulled in so many different directions and tasked with so many responsibilities that I had trouble just trying to make sense of it all. Just as I would get one thing done, three more things would fall onto my plate, and, of course, they all needed to be done right away, if not sooner. I was living a hectic and chaotic life in which there weren't enough hours in the day or enough days in the week to get everything done that needed to be done. I was falling further behind with each passing day, and there didn't seem to be any relief in sight.

And so, with much angst and consternation, I made the rather difficult decision to skip archery season. I figured that if I skip archery season, I could use the months of October and November to dig myself out of my current schedule predicament and maybe, just maybe, get a few days of rifle hunting in come December. I reasoned that this plan would still give me an opportunity to get a buck this year; it would just have to be with the rifle instead of the bow. Again, this wasn't a decision that I liked, but I felt that it was what I had to do. In reality, I didn't have much of a choice in the matter; life was just way too out of control to do any archery hunting this year.

And so, when the opening day of archery season rolled around, instead of heading out for a leisurely morning in the stand, I busily contented myself with the chores of the day. This was all well and good for a while, but as the leaves started to fall and signs of the rut began to emerge, I seriously started to regret my decision to skip archery season. With each passing day, I felt an increasingly greater desire to be in the woods as I grew ever more frustrated with my circumstances.

By November 6th I had reached my breaking point. I had been going hardcore for the past two months and needed a change of perspective. Knowing that the rut was in full swing and that there was still one more week of archery season left, I said to heck with it all and made the decision to go archery hunting.

I hadn't done any scouting or practice shooting, but I generally hunt in the same area on the farm behind my house and three quick shots with the crossbow proved that it was dead on. I was ready to hunt, and the next morning found me perched high in my favorite white oak well before daylight.

It felt good to be in the woods. My mind wasn't racing back and forth between the intense combination of schedules, budgets, and deadlines that had been so demanding here of late. I had no earthly expectations for actually getting a deer and was just happy to be out enjoying the sights and sounds of God's natural creation. I already felt blessed for the opportunity and was thoroughly enjoying every minute of it.

About an hour after sunrise, I caught movement off to my right and spotted two yearling does bounding up through the woods. They eventually stopped running and started to browse on the brushy vegetation about 65 yards out from my stand. I thought it odd that these deer came running up from the bottom, but then stopped to feed in an unconcerned manner. If they had been spooked by another hunter they probably would've kept running for cover. It was almost as if another deer had run them out of the bottom.

Less than ten minutes later, another yearling, this time a small button buck, came running up from the bottom and proceeded to bed down about 50 yards behind me. Now I was convinced that these yearlings were being run off by another deer, most likely a rutting buck, and I kept my eyes peeled for any movement whatsoever. If there was a rut-crazed buck in the area, I wanted to be ready for it.

It didn't take long before I saw deer moving in the thick brush down below my stand. I couldn't tell for sure, but I got a very distinct feeling that it was a buck chasing a doe. Since they didn't come out of the brush, I decided to try calling to them. The combination of an estrus bleat and a buck grunt can be very effective at luring deer at this time of year, and I decided to give it a try. My series of grunts and bleats didn't garner an immediate response like I was hoping for; it took almost ten minutes for the buck to come investigate. When this bruiser 8-point came trotting out of the brush, I nearly gasped in wide-eyed amazement. It was one of the biggest bucks that I've ever seen while out hunting, and I could barely believe my eyes. When he turned and started heading in my direction, I could feel myself getting weak in the knees. I distinctly remember thinking to myself that this is going to happen, and it's going to happen now, so don't blow it.

With the buck standing broadside at 30 yards, I steadied the crosshairs just behind the shoulder and gently squeezed the trigger. The arrow hit the deer with a noticeable thud, and he immediately sprang into action. I could clearly see blood pouring out of him as he ran down past my stand and disappeared back into the brush from where he came. I thought I heard him fall about 20 yards into the brush, but I wasn't sure.

The commotion of the wounded buck running back into the brush was enough to spook the doe that he was chasing, and she came running out into the open just below my stand. Eventually, she headed up through the woods, and I sat back down to contemplate what had just happened. I had just shot the biggest buck of my life and had done it in less than two hours of hunting on my first morning in the woods. This was all a little too unreal, and I needed some time to process it.

In looking down through the woods, I could see a clear blood trail leading all the way into the brush where he disappeared. I felt relatively confident that the buck was down, but the shot was further back than I would've liked, and I didn't want to push him. Instead of potentially losing the biggest buck of my life by doing something stupid, I decided to play it safe and give him plenty of time. To that end, I quietly climbed down out of the tree and snuck out of the woods to go home for a while. This isn't what I wanted to do, I wanted to go start looking for him right away, but I figured it would be better to be safe than sorry.

After two nail-biting hours, I eased my way back into the woods to start looking for him. With God's good grace, the search only took a few minutes as I found him lying dead right where I thought I heard him fall. There was a heavy blood trail leading all the way up to him, and it was clear that he had expired quickly. The arrow placement was less than perfect, but it still proved to be effective; he only went about 70 yards from where I shot him.

In looking him over more closely, I found that he only had a 14-inch inside spread, but his G2's measured upwards of 9 inches. This was a dandy buck, a Pennsylvania wall hanger if there ever was one, and I was absolutely dumbfounded by it all. God had blessed me with a trophy buck, the biggest of my 20-year hunting career, and I had put virtually no effort into it. It was as if it was meant to be, a true blessing from above – a gift from the Lord to ease my frantic soul, and I thanked Him profusely for it.

I ended up going back to work the next day, but all the schedules, budgets, and deadlines seemed a little less daunting with the thought of that big blessing buck still fresh in my mind. For I had just been reminded, in a very tangible and rewarding way, that God is always providing for me, He knows exactly what we need and when we need it, and that all things are possible through Him…a blessing buck indeed!

Undeserving

I had no earthly expectations for shooting a deer when I left the house on that cold, November morning. In fact, I was of the mindset that I really didn't deserve one, especially after what had happened the week before. However, the rut was on, and the weather was looking pretty good; so I decided to head out and spend a couple hours in the stand to see if anything was moving.

As I sat there in the dark waiting for the sun to rise, I couldn't help but to think back to the previous Friday evening and how badly I messed things up. I had decided to do an evening hunt because I wasn't seeing much in the way of deer movement during the previous three mornings in the stand. Besides, I was in the mood to try something different and figured there was nothing to lose but time.

As the evening slowly faded into darkness, I heard something coming from my left and was surprised to find a small 8-point stepping out of the brush less than 25 yards away. Through the binoculars I could see that it was a legal buck, but the sun had already set, and it was really starting to get dark. I needed him to come 10 yards closer to get a clear shot, but I was down to the wire in regard to legal shooting time.

When he finally cleared the brush and turned broadside, I steadied the 20-yard reticle of my crossbow just behind his shoulder and gently squeezed the trigger. It was too dark to shoot, and I knew it, but, in my overzealous desire to get a deer, I let an arrow fly anyway. I could still see the buck, but what I couldn't see was the single tree branch that deflected the arrow low into the deer's body.

At the shot, the buck sprang into action and ran 30 yards behind me and stopped. Not knowing what had happened, he just stood there trying to figure things out.

It was at this point in the evening that I heard another deer approaching from the same direction that the first had come, and I looked down through the woods to find a much bigger 8-point headed straight towards me. This 8-point was a bruiser buck with heavy, sweeping main beams and good tines. I didn't need binoculars to see that this was a legal buck; he was a real dandy. This big 8-point came within 10 yards of my stand and started to feed on the woody browse. All the while, I was trying to stay intently focused on what was going on back behind me in hopeful anticipation that the buck I had just shot would fall over dead at any second. Unfortunately, that didn't happen, and when he took off down through the woods at a good clip, I could feel my heart sink down into my gut.

I sat in the stand for another 15 minutes waiting for the big 8 to walk away, but he showed no signs of leaving. I eventually spooked him off as I was packing up my gear to climb down.

When I found the arrow, it confirmed what I had been fearing – a brisket shot with gristly fat on the arrow and white belly fur on the ground. I found a small pool of blood where the buck had been standing, but it wasn't a lot of blood for how long he stood there.

I decided to back out and give the deer some time before I picked up the blood trail. Two hours later and with reinforcements having been called in, my dad and I started off down the blood trail hoping to find the buck lying dead at every step along the way. We trailed that deer in the pitch-black darkness for nearly 400 yards all the way down to the creek before we lost blood. At 10:00 P.M. we decided to call it a night and try again in the morning.

After a long, sleepless night, I headed out at first light to look for sign down by the creek, but I found nothing. Unlike the deer, the trail died at the creek, and the buck disappeared into oblivion. I scoured the creek banks for hundreds of yards trying to find where he got out, but it was useless. He was gone, and I had to accept the bitter fact that I made a poor shot and lost him because of it. It was a bad deal all the way around, and I felt horrible about it.

Archery hunters take comfort in telling themselves that it happens to everyone at some point in their hunting career, but I knew that it was too dark when I pulled the trigger. This was 100% my fault, my stupid mistake, and now a deer was wounded, if not dead, because of it. Further, I had thoroughly spooked a magnificent buck (i.e., the big 8-point) that would probably now never be seen again. A bad deal indeed.

All of this was being replayed in my mind as I sat there in the dark waiting for the sun to rise. I tried to tell myself that that all happened a week ago and that today was a new day in which I could redeem myself by doing everything right, but I still felt very undeserving to even be in the woods, much less shoot another deer.

At 7:30 I was still wallowing in my remorse when I heard a deer walking out in front of me. It was headed in my direction, and I spotted him just as he was emerging from the brush. To my astonishment, it was the big 8-point, the one with heavy, sweeping main beams and good tines. I couldn't believe it. With all the ruckus I caused last week, I figured this deer would've been in the next county by now, but here he was less than 15 yards away and getting closer. Instinct, borne out of two decades of archery hunting, took over, and I immediately got ready to shoot.

Cognizant of the desire to avoid a repeat performance, I confirmed that there were no unforeseen obstacles in the way, and when he turned broadside at 12 yards, I let him have it. The arrow placement was perfect, and the buck took off on a dead run. I say dead run because that's what he was; he just didn't know it yet.

As I sat in the stand thinking about what had just happened, I felt a sense of peace settle over me. I was completely and totally undeserving of a blessing such as this, but then I remembered that there is another blessing, a much greater gift, that I am also completely and totally undeserving of. As a sinner, I am completely and totally undeserving of an eternal life in heaven, but that didn't stop Jesus from paying the price for me. Through the atoning sacrifice of His precious blood, I have been made righteous in the eyes of the Lord and am destined to spend eternity in His holy presence. That's as good as it gets, and I did nothing to deserve it.

With a renewed spirit of excitement and an intensely humble feeling of appreciation, I climbed down out of the stand and took up the blood trail. It was easy to follow, and I found the big 8 lying dead within a hundred yards. On bended knee, I praised the Good Lord for letting me find this buck, for giving me another chance, and for allowing me to experience such an awesome blessing, however undeserving I may be.

Second-Chance Tom

Getting a second chance at any trophy game animal is a rare thing, but it's almost unheard of when it comes to spring gobbler hunting. To put it quite simply, big toms don't get big by being dumb. Rather, they get big by being extremely smart and wary. They know how to avoid hunters and stay alive despite our use of realistic calls and lifelike decoys. I don't know if it's inherited or learned, but such gobblers can be extremely difficult, if not impossible, to kill. Even less endowed and less educated birds can still be hard to kill. Therefore, most turkey hunters know that it's a special gift to get a shot at a big tom and that they better not blow it because the likelihood of getting another shot at that same bird in the same season is extraordinarily low.

Being fully cognizant of this basic turkey hunting precept, I never could've predicted the outcome of the 2016 Spring Gobbler Season and am still in relative shock at how it all played out. In typical God's Country Naturalist fashion, I started my preseason scouting in early April, nearly a month before the actual hunting season, and by the time opening day rolled around, I had managed to find multiple gobblers at four different spots all within close proximity to my southcentral Pennsylvania residence.

Never before did I have so many valid, high-probability hunting options from which to choose, and I had some degree of difficulty in trying to decide which spot to focus on. For all intents and purposes, the 2016 Spring Gobbler Season was looking to be a good one, and I had high hopes for scoring on a big longbeard once the season started.

Needless to say, sleep did not come easy the night before the season opener.

Unfortunately, this is where things started to go down hill. I awoke at 3:30 A.M. on the morning of the opening day to find less-than-ideal hunting conditions. It was damp and rainy down in the farm country and cold and foggy up in the mountains. Further, I soon learned that the big tom I was planning to hunt decided to move the day before and was now roosted several hundred yards onto a neighboring property that I don't have permission to hunt. Consequently, the opening day came and went, and I didn't even come close to working a bird. For what had every possibility of being an exceptional day in the field, the first day of the 2016 Spring Gobbler Season ended up being a total flop, at least for me anyway.

Returning home at lunchtime, I remember pulling into the driveway feeling rather dejected about the whole affair. Luckily, I had made arrangements to take some time off work the first week of the season, and it looked like I was going to need it.

After the opening day debacle, I did some serious strategizing about my upcoming game plan, but eventually decided to go back to where I started hunting first thing Saturday morning. The longbeard that I had been seeing at that location was a magnificent bird, and I wanted to give him another try. Maybe this time he would be roosted in his normal spot, and I could have a go at him.

If the opening day was less than stellar, I would soon learn that the first Monday of the season would prove to be an even worse experience. As planned, I was set up and in position well before daylight on this, the second day of the season, when I was pleased to hear that the big tom had indeed returned to his normal roost spot on the property that I have permission to hunt.

With this first obstacle working out in my favor, it was now time to let him know that I was there, and I proceeded to issue the most seductive series of tree yelps that I could muster with my diaphragm call. He responded back immediately with a terrific gobble, and I knew I was in business.

Over the course of the next 15 minutes, we exchanged pleasantries half a dozen more times, and when he finally decided to fly down, I got the gun up and got ready. He immediately started to close the 150-yard distance between us, and within a matter of minutes, I was watching him in full strut out in the field in front of me.

My setup had worked perfectly, and this old tom was about to take a dirt nap. With the camouflaged barrel of my high-end turkey gun steadily trained on his neck, I pulled the trigger and broke the morning peace. Mentally, I had already filled out the tag and was beginning to wonder if I had enough time to make it back home to show the gobbler to my wife before she left for work.

You can imagine my surprise when I looked out into the field and didn't see my gobbler crumpled in the dirt. Instead, he was standing there perfectly unscathed, but on full alert regarding what had just happened. Apparently, I missed! There's a first time for everything, and this was my first time for missing a turkey. This painful reality was not well received, and I watched in stupefied disbelief as he quickly disappeared back into the woods from which he came. You don't get many opportunities at big gobblers like that, and I totally blew it. The disappointment was crushing, and that's putting it mildly.

After regaining my composure, I tried to assess what went wrong and eventually came to the conclusion that I misjudged the distance. What I thought to be roughly a 40-yard shot ended up being almost 60 yards. Being out in an open field with no frame of reference with which to judge distance, the gobbler ended up being a lot farther away than I realized, and my gun just couldn't cover that distance. I followed up in the woods to make sure that he wasn't injured and hiding in the brush somewhere, but that proved to be a wasted effort. I missed, and that's all there was to it.

Once again, I returned home feeling rather dejected about the whole affair, but this dejection was significantly worse than before. For all I knew, that big longbeard was probably so freaked out that he wouldn't gobble again the rest of the season. I severely doubted that he would be huntable again. Needless to say, I was now second guessing everything that I did and spent the rest of the day thinking about what I should've done differently. In other words, I spent the rest of the day wallowing in self-pity.

Moving on, I wasn't able to hunt the next two days due to some unavoidable work obligations, but I was back out again on Thursday morning more out of curiosity than anything. I wanted to know if that tom would still be roosted in his normal spot and if he would do any gobbling. Admittedly, I held little hope for either of these things, but I wanted to know.

To my surprise, he was roosted exactly where he was three days ago and he was gobbling. I was even more surprised when he hammered back at my series of yelps. This old boy was hot, and I started to think that I might just get a second chance at him. Instead of setting up in the field though, I decided to close the distance myself this morning. I wanted to hunt him in the woods closer to where he was roosted. With all of the emerging vegetation in the woods, I was able to sneak to within 80 yards of where he was roosted and got set up next to a big oak tree.

He stayed on the roost a little longer this morning, but he was answering all of my calls with thunderous gobbles. When he finally flew down, he started working in my direction immediately, and I was ready for him. At 40 yards, he gobbled right in front of me, but I still couldn't see him. At 25 yards, he broke through the brush and came into full view. I let him close the distance to 18 yards, and when he stopped to look around, I let him have it. There was no missing this time; he dropped in his tracks.

I couldn't believe what had just happened. For some miraculous and inexplicable reason, the Good Lord had blessed me with a second-chance tom, and what a gobbler it was. Weighing in at 21.5 pounds and sporting a 9.5-inch beard, he was everything that I thought he was. I knew he was a great bird, but after missing him on Monday, I figured it was pretty much over for the season. In all honesty, I didn't even expect to see him again, much less get another shot at him. It goes without saying that I returned home that morning feeling quite different from that of the previous two hunts. A second-chance tom is an awesome thing, and I felt extremely blessed for having been granted such a gift.

Later that day, I was reflecting on the morning's good fortune when it occurred to me that redemption in the turkey woods is not the only second chance that the Good Lord has afforded me. As awesome as a second-chance gobbler may be, it pales in comparison to the second chance at life that comes by way of forgiveness through the cross and putting our trust and faith in Jesus. For as the bible affirms, God loves us so much that he was willing to send His one and only son, such that whoever believes in Him will not perish, but have eternal life (John 3:16). That's the greatest second chance that there is, and all who believe should feel extremely blessed for having been granted such a wonderful gift.

Wiping the Slate Clean

Sometimes things just don't go the way they're supposed to in the great outdoors. It doesn't matter how much you plan or how hard you try, some days it's just not meant to be. This applies to both hunting and fishing endeavors, which require a certain degree of skill combined with just the right amount of luck in order to be successful on any given outing. When either one of these things is missing or lacking, the likelihood for a successful day in the field decreases exponentially. This is not to say that it won't still be a good day in the field; it just might not be a successful day in the field, and every sportsman knows that these are two very different things.

If, however, your primary objective for a particular outing is to be successful and it simply isn't happening for whatever reason, maybe a fresh start is needed. Perhaps the opportunity to regroup and/or refocus your efforts (i.e., to wipe the slate clean and start over) could make all the difference in the world in regard to the success of the outing. Again, this applies to both hunting and fishing endeavors, which have the potential to be positively impacted by starting over with a fresh, refocused effort. If nothing else, the renewed energy and enthusiasm that typically accompanies a fresh start can make for a better time afield regardless of the level of success.

This concept of starting over with a regrouped and/or refocused effort paid off in a big way for me during the 2017 Spring Gobbler Season. It was the second day of the season, and I was looking to score on one of the big longbeards that are known to frequent the woods on the farm behind my house. I archery hunt for deer in this patch of woods and saw some really nice gobblers there back in November. I didn't know if they would be there on this particular morning, but I figured I would give it a try and see what happens.

At first light, a lone gobbler sounded off from somewhere down in the creek bottom, and I hustled down through the woods to get into position for what could be a flash hunt. Unfortunately, this bird showed no interest in my calls and proceeded to fly down and disappear. I never even got a chance to really work this bird. I'm not sure what his deal was, but he didn't want to have anything to do with me, and he made that pretty obvious.

This was a disappointing start to the morning, but I didn't let it get to me. This bird wasn't interested in playing ball, but I knew he wasn't the only game in town. There are a number of nice longbeards in this general vicinity, so I decided to do a little running and gunning to find a more accommodating gobbler. This is not an uncommon practice in the world of spring gobbler hunting. When the birds in one area aren't cooperating, most diehard turkey hunters start covering ground in order to find a more responsive gobbler. Such a strategy is a proven method for increasing one's chances of success when you can't work a bird off the roost first thing in the morning.

Unfortunately, four hours and several exhausting miles later, I still hadn't come close to working a bird. In fact, I couldn't even find another bird, much less one that was interested in anything that I had to offer. This was really starting to turn into a disappointing morning, so I decided to head back home and weigh my options. Besides, I was getting quite thirsty and needed something to drink. Several hours of hiking around in the warm May sun with nothing to drink was starting to take its toll on me, and I had no desire to press on without first getting hydrated.

After a refreshing glass of water and several minutes of contemplative rest, I felt much more inclined to continue with the hunt. Mentally, I needed this little break to reassess the situation. Now I was reenergized, reorganized, and refocused. I was ready to wipe the morning hunt off the books and get on with a fresh start.

To that end, I decided to go back to where I started hunting first thing in the morning. It was the only spot that I heard a gobbler all morning, so I figured it would be my best option. My plan was to set up in the area where I typically hunt deer and call every ten minutes or so until quitting time at noon. It was only 10:15 A.M., so I had plenty of time to call one in, if there was one that was willing to be called in. If not, it would still make for a peaceful, relaxing time in the woods enjoying God's natural creation, and there's no downside to that.

With my decoys deployed, I sat down at the base of a big oak tree and proceeded to issue a series of yelps with my box call. I was more than a bit surprised when a distant gobbler responded in turn. This bird was a long way off, but I'm pretty sure he gobbled to the sound of that box call.

Hitting it again, the gobbler fired back in response. This is when I switched over to a slate call and started to do some high-pitched cutting. The gobbler fired back again, but he was still way off in the distance. This back and forth exchange went on for the better part of 45 minutes, during which time he was continuously getting closer. I was eventually able to call him all the way up the creek bottom to the point that he was just down the hill and across the creek from me. And by "he", I should clarify that I really mean "they" because it was two longbeards that came in together. I have no idea how far those birds came, but I'm guessing that it was somewhere in the neighborhood of three-quarters-of-a-mile. When I first sat down and started calling, their gobbles were just barely perceptible in the remote distance. I really didn't think that they would come all that way, but they most certainly did, and now I needed to get them to cross the creek for me.

In order to do that, I worked them up into a gobbling frenzy and then went quiet on them. It worked like a charm. By going quiet, the gobblers thought their "hen" was losing interest and moving off. They didn't want that, so they took matters into their own hands and flew across the creek to check things out. The next time I called, the gobblers were just down the hill from me and closing fast. At 20 yards, I could hear one spitting and drumming, but still couldn't see them through the thick multi-flora rose. When they finally came walking out of the brush at a mere 12 yards, I put the bead of my shotgun on the neck of the strutter and pulled the trigger.

It was 11:15 in the morning, and I had just finished my 2017 Spring Gobbler Season with a textbook-perfect, mid-morning hunt. This 21.5-pound, 10-inch longbeard stud felt quite hefty hanging over my shoulder as I carried him out of the woods. Clearly, my decision to go home, get refreshed, and then start over with a refocused effort was a major factor in the cause of this unexpected success. By wiping the slate clean on a dismal early morning hunt and starting over with renewed interest and enthusiasm on a mid-morning hunt, I was able to turn the ever-fickle tide of success in my favor. This doesn't always happen so easily, but when it does, the reward is super sweet, like tagging out on the second day of the season with a trophy longbeard.

That's about as good as it gets when it comes to spring gobbler hunting.

As much as this concept of starting over with a clean slate applies to hunting and fishing endeavors, it has even greater applicability for those who have placed their trust and faith in Jesus. As followers of Christ, we acknowledge God's loving sacrifice on the cross and the fact that Jesus willingly laid down his life to pay the price for our sins and transgressions. In so doing, Jesus has wiped the slate clean for us and given us a fresh start at life; a new or reborn life in which we can find peace, love, joy, happiness, and contentment by knowing God as our father and Jesus as our savior.

This is, most assuredly, the absolute best kind of starting over that there is or ever possibly could be for us on this earth. And the best part of it all is that this kind of starting over is guaranteed to result in success because if we choose to walk in faith with Jesus, He will, most assuredly, choose to walk with us too. In fact, He will carry us when we most need Him. Surely, it doesn't get any better than that!

A Wood Duck Odyssey

I quit! I've had enough, and I'm officially throwing in the towel. I don't want to have anything else to do with it. I'm done, and that's all there is to it. I don't particularly like going out this way, but it is what it is, and there's not much I can do about it. It's over, I'm admitting my defeat, and I'm moving on. There will be no more duck hunting for me.

Generally speaking, I am not a waterfowl hunter. It's not that I have anything against it (even though I am an avid bird watcher); it's just never really been my thing. For whatever reason, I've always tended to gravitate towards deer hunting and turkey hunting and never had much of an interest in duck hunting.

This all changed a couple years ago, however, when I started to notice the wood ducks that were hanging out in the creek bottom down below my house. I have permission to hunt deer in this creek bottom and was seeing wood ducks quite regularly as I was coming and going during the archery deer season. Having always considered the male wood duck to be the prettiest duck on the planet, I eventually talked myself into trying to get one.

Inevitably, I suspect that I would've gotten it mounted if I had been successful in shooting one, but that never came to fruition. For various and sundry reasons, I could never close the deal on that coveted drake woodie, and the epic failure of this most recent duck season was the straw that finally broke the camel's back (and just to be clear, the camel's back to which I am referring is meant to be symbolic of my desire to continue in the act of wood duck hunting).

Leading up to this most recent season, my wood duck hunting experiences had consisted of the most deplorable array of errant misdemeanors and demeaning errors, the likes of which would've driven even the most-hearty souls to seek out mental counseling. From missed shots to nearly getting shot myself, my duck hunting history has been less than stellar, and that's putting it mildly. Suffice it to say, a better man would've seen the light and quit while he was ahead, but I am blind in one eye and have never really been able to see all that well out of the other, hence my steadfast determination regarding the matter.

In strategizing my attack strategy, I decided that the use of extremely lifelike decoys was no longer the pathway to success when it comes to getting a wood duck. I had been using these decoys for the previous three seasons, and the ducks payed no attention to them whatsoever. They would fly right over them and keep going straight up the creek. It was almost as if the decoys were driving the ducks away, which, of course, is not the desired effect of a decoy.

Therefore, I decided that my attack strategy for this upcoming season would consist of stalking the creek banks and jump shooting the ducks as they fly away. All of the hunting literature that I had read recommended this strategy as being the most successful technique for consistently shooting wood ducks. It certainly sounded like a plausible method that could lead to success, but the literature failed to mention that wood ducks have a miraculous ability to disappear. I had to learn that on my own.

Dressed from head to toe in high-definition camouflage, I carefully inched my way down the creek glassing every nook and cranny as I went. I had only gone about 50 yards when I spotted a beautiful drake and two hen woodies feeding on acorns along the opposite bank. So far as I could tell, they hadn't seen me and didn't appear to be alarmed in any way. I watched them through the binoculars for several minutes, and when they disappeared behind a small island, I quickly hustled into position to get ready for the shot. I could clearly see both upstream and downstream of the island and was ready to shoot regardless of which end they emerged. It was just a waiting game at this point.

After all of my duck hunting troubles, I could hardly believe that it was going to be this simple. I had this drake completely pinned down, and success was all but imminent. I wasn't even going to let him fly. The second I spotted him emerge from behind the island, I was going to kill him. I wasn't going to risk the possibility of missing him in the air. This drake was mine, and I earned it. Shooting him in the air or on the water made no difference to me at all; I was going to be completely happy either way.

As the seconds faded into minutes and then tens of minutes, I started to get a little antsy for them to emerge. I knew they were there and that they had no place to go, so I just needed to be patient and wait them out. I told myself that it would all be worth it – the many days of early morning wake-ups, the pre-dawn set ups, the disappointing misses, the close calls, and the long walks back home – once I finally laid my hands on that magnificent drake.

After 30 minutes, I couldn't take it anymore and decided to walk up on the island to see what was going on. I was fully ready to shoot the drake in the air if I accidentally flushed him in the process. Quietly stepping onto the island, I peeked over the edge hoping to see the tops of their heads, but I couldn't. Another step allowed me to see even more of the opposite side, but there was still nothing. With nothing to lose at this point, I went for it and cleared the island. Jumping into the creek on the opposite side, my gun was shouldered and ready for action, but there was nothing. They were gone. There were no ducks anywhere.

Humility, gained through a lifetime of humbling experiences, allows me to admit that I have been dumbfounded on more than one occasion, but this one was downright baffling. It was a true Elmer Fudd moment. I stood there in the middle of that creek having absolutely no clue as to where those ducks went or how they did it. I know they went behind the island, but I never saw them come back out and I could see three sides of it. Logic would dictate that they had to be on the fourth side, which is exactly where I saw them go when I made my move to get into shooting position. To this day, I still can't figure out where those ducks went. It's like they disappeared down a hole or vanished into thin air. It is, by far, the closest thing I've ever seen to a paranormal phenomenon, which I don't believe in.

Regardless of where they went or how they did it, I was thoroughly duped by a trio of birds with brains the size of a lima bean. Defeated was the only word that could accurately describe how I felt. It was at this point that I finally came to my senses and admitted that I am just not meant to be a duck hunter. I'm no good at it, and I have no reason to believe that I would ever get any better at it. It's not that I'm a quitter, but you gotta know when you're beat at something. As previously stated, I don't particularly like going out this way, but it is what it is, and there's not much I can do about it. There's no point to floundering in your defeat. There are bigger fish to fry in this world, and I'm moving on to something I'm more suited for. It's that simple.

In a similar manner, God has blessed each and every one of us with a special gift - a personal talent - that can be used to advance His kingdom while we are here on earth. Sometimes this gift is obvious and certain people know exactly what it is and how they're supposed to use it, but more often that's not the case. In most instances, it seems to be a lot easier to figure out the things in life that we aren't so blessed in. We shouldn't be discouraged by this though. Seeking God's purpose for our life is a good thing, and there's a very real possibility that we may be living out that purpose without even knowing it. Only in the fullness of time will our gift and ultimate purpose in life be revealed to us.

As for me, I think it's pretty safe to assume that my divine talent in life has nothing to do with duck hunting. I guess I'll just have to keep searching.

A Fishing Miscellany

Farm Ponds and Four-Year-Olds

Some matches really do seem to be made in heaven, like a perfect combination rendered by God's own hand. The combinations of Adam and Eve, bow and arrow, and flint and steel are just a couple examples of these perfect pairs. In each of these instances, you simply can't have the one without the other; they were just made to go together. Of course, in the case of Adam and Eve, they were directly rendered by God's own hand and made to go together, thus resulting in a truly perfect pair.

Another God-given combination that I discovered while out fishing with my daughter is that of farm ponds and four-year-olds. You wouldn't think it at first, they're not a readily evident pair, but, when it comes to teaching a kid how to fish, farm ponds and four-year-olds just seem to go together. It's as if the one was made for the other – a perfect combination rendered by God's own hand.

Generally speaking, most farm ponds contain a healthy supply of ready and willing panfish (i.e., bluegills, sunfish, crappies, etc.) that are eager to take a youngster's bait, thereby resulting in a high success, high frequency catch rate that is typically adequate to hold a young person's attention for more than just a couple minutes. Second, and perhaps more important, is the undeniable fact that kids love to go fishing, especially with their dad. It was the realization of these two fundamental truths that led to the discovery of the perfect combination that is farm ponds and four-year-olds.

In looking back on it, I think the first farm pond outing with my four-year-old daughter, Megan, was the most memorable. Living in the country as we do, we have been granted permission to fish in our neighbor's pond, which is conveniently located just down the road from our house. This first outing was kind of a spur-of-the-moment type affair, and we weren't prepared with any sort of traditional bait. As a result, we ended up swiping a bag of miniature marshmallows from the kitchen pantry and beating a hasty retreat down to the pond before my wife could catch us.

Outfitted with a pink Barbie fishing rod and a plastic bobber, we hit the pond in high style for our first fishing lesson. It took a little bit of coaxing, but once the bluegills figured out that marshmallows are edible, they were all over them. Meg proved herself to be a natural at setting the hook and had no problem fighting each fish in with her little kiddie rod. Everything was going great right up until Meg ate the bait, thus putting a rather abrupt end to our first fishing session.

Despite the apparent bait issues, this first outing proved to be very successful. Meg caught her first fish, she learned some of the basics of fishing, and we both had a wonderful time in the process...a tremendous success indeed!

We were much more prepared for our second outing, and the results showed it. Armed with a dozen lively nightcrawlers, Meg nearly tripled her catch of bluegills and added her first bass to the tally, a fine largemouth in the 13-inch class. The bass was an unexpected catch and proved to be quite sporting on her little pink rod. Fortunately, Meg's angling skills were no match for this fish, and she landed it in short order. It was a fantastic experience, and we both enjoyed it thoroughly.

I was quickly coming to realize that fishing is an excellent means for spending time outdoors with my daughter introducing her to the wonders and mysteries of

God's natural creation, which is something that I had been working at since the day she was born. Only now, however, was the act of fishing finally becoming one of the primary methods for accomplishing this. I had long dreamed of taking my one and only child fishing, and that was now evolving into an awesome reality.

Throughout the remainder of that summer, Meg and I paid several more visits to the local farm pond, and each one proved to be time well spent. We even had a couple nighttime fishing adventures using lighted bobbers, during which she was successful in catching a number of sizeable catfish (or "whisker fish" as she took to calling them).

Since that time, we have branched out to try other fishing venues, including stream fishing for trout and saltwater fishing for stripers, and have been remarkably successful in those endeavors, but they weren't quite the same as that first year of farm pond outings. I think it was the initial newness of it all, combined with the opportunity to teach her about something that I really enjoy, that made that first year of farm pond outings so fun and memorable. I know neither of us will ever forget some of those wonderful experiences down at the pond.

Of course, teaching my daughter how to fish (as fun as that may be) pales in comparison to my other fatherly responsibilities to set a good example, to live a godly life, and to teach her about our lord and savior Jesus Christ. These things are of a significantly greater importance for her as they have the potential to help guide and shape her future Christian faith. While I sometimes fail at living up to these responsibilities, they are, nonetheless, my burden to bear, and I strive to do my absolute best at each one of them. With a little help from above, I pray that Meg will grow to love the Lord with all her heart, mind, and soul and that she will learn to fully appreciate all the good things that God's natural creation has to offer. Further, I hope that, in some small capacity, the memories of her farm pond days with dad will help to bring about both of these things. Nothing would please me more!

Chasing Kings and Chrome

When it comes to fishing, nothing beats the lure-crushing strikes and rod-punishing runs of a king salmon caught on light tackle. The ensuing fight is an equally matched battle of wills that can, and often does, go on for several minutes, until such time that the fish begins to tire and can gradually be worked in towards the boat. Even then, they typically make one or more boatside runs in a last-ditch effort to avoid the net. In comparing it to other outdoor activities, I rank salmon fishing right up there with spring gobbler hunting and archery hunting during the rut; it's that much fun.

If there's a close second in the realm of big game sportfishing, it would have to be the steelhead. Hooking up with fresh chrome (i.e., a bright silver steelhead just in from the lake or ocean) in a fast-flowing river or stream can result in a rod-bending, reel-screaming battle similar to that of a big king. Any disadvantage in size that a steelhead may have relative to a salmon, they certainly make up for in visual appearance and physical temperament.

Apart from being an absolutely gorgeous fish, steelhead are notorious fighters, one of the strongest in freshwater. Consequently, everyone knows that just because you hook a steelhead, doesn't mean that you're actually going to land a steelhead. Given their legendary tenacity, it's just as probable that they will either throw the hook or break the line before they're ever brought to hand.

What's even better about salmon and steelhead is that they're often found together in the same rivers and streams. Salmon migrate up the rivers they were born in to spawn, and the steelhead follow close behind to feed on the fresh salmon eggs. As a result, many streams that experience one or more runs of salmon also receive a subsequent run of steelhead, thus rendering these particular rivers and streams doubly blessed.

Being such highly prized sportfish, fishermen from all over the world travel hundreds, if not thousands, of miles to experience the thrill of catching them. Major destinations that have the potential to fulfill this dream include such storied places as the Kamchatka Peninsula in eastern Russia, coastal Alaska, British Columbia, the Pacific Northwest, and a number of the Great Lakes tributary streams. While I would love to fish some of these more remote and prestigious destinations, I consider myself fortunate to have the opportunity to fish several of the Great Lakes tributary streams on what seems to have become an annual basis.

Every fall for the past several years, I've been making the drive up to Oswego County, New York to fish for salmon and steelhead in Lake Ontario and several of its tributary waters. These New York fishing trips have grown to become the hallmark events of my annual outdoor calendar, and I look forward to them immensely.

Starting in early October, I make my first trip up to New York to fish exclusively for salmon. We generally target pre-spawn fish that are staging in the relatively shallow water of Lake Ontario near the mouth of the Salmon River. Fishing at night in a drift boat, we troll glow spoons under the cover of darkness searching for big kings that are willing to bite.

Many people think that salmon fishing means snagging, and there are a lot of unethical snaggers out there, but there is absolutely no snagging involved in this type of fishing. We fish for biters (fish that strike lures out of sheer aggression), and there's nothing quite like it when a 20-pound king attacks a glow spoon. The rod doubles over completely parallel with the boat, and the fight is on. Depending on the size of the fish, it could take upwards of ten minutes to land, and it's an arm-tiring brawl the entire time. When that big king is finally thrashing his last inside the net, I am often struck by an overwhelming feeling of excitement and prideful accomplishment, most likely driven by the rush of adrenaline that is coursing through my body as a result of what just happened. There's no doubt about it, catching trophy king salmon at night while trolling glow spoons from a drift boat in Lake Ontario is about as fun as it gets.

There are, however, a number of other viable methods and means for catching big kings, and one in particular stands out. It takes the right kind of water under the right conditions, but it is possible to catch salmon by casting deep-diving crankbaits. This is not a common or even widely known way of catching salmon, but it can be effective when the fish are holding in deeper water.

Case in point, we were fishing the lower end of the Oswego River early one morning when my guide suggested that we try throwing deep-diving crankbaits. I was skeptical at first, but after several lure changes, we found a color pattern that was sufficiently agitating to entice a fish to strike.

While slowly retrieving a yellow Thunderstick, I had a fish slam the lure and take off running. The strike was so fast and violent that it almost ripped the rod right out of my hands. This big hen was absolutely infuriated and took off on a reel-screaming run the second she was hooked. She peeled more than a hundred feet of line off the reel before I was able to get her stopped and turned around. I knew that

I was dealing with a bruiser fish and that I had my work cut out for me. When she finally stopped running, I laid into her with as much tension as the line could handle. As suspected, it was a back and forth battle of minor advances followed by line-striping runs that would undue my minor advances.

After ten nail-biting minutes, I was finally able to work this 40-inch, 25-pound king into the net. It was at this point that I came to the full realization that the Good Lord had just gifted me with an absolute monster of a fish, my largest king salmon to date, and I sincerely thanked Him for it. It was an awesome experience catching a fish of this caliber, especially on a hand-casted crankbait. This is the kind of thing that many fishermen only dream about, and here I was living it. Needless to say, I returned home from that trip feeling quite blessed.

Six weeks later, I was back up in Oswego County for another fishing adventure, but this time it was to chase steelhead in the Salmon River. Floating down the Salmon River in a drift boat on a cold, November morning is an adventure in and of itself. Throw in a couple energetic steelhead, and it makes for a truly unforgettable experience.

Setting off down the Salmon River at first light, we methodically worked each hole and run using a combination of different colored egg sacks and Trick Em' beads suspended under a float. The fish were far and few between, but we managed to tangle with enough of them to render the trip a blazing success. Over the course of two days, I had the immense privilege of hooking up with eight steelhead. What's even more amazing is that I managed to land all eight of them without losing a single fish. That's somewhat unprecedented when it comes to fresh steelhead.

Needless to say, I returned home from New York once again feeling quite blessed.

Back-to-back trips yielding an impressive number of trophy salmon and steelhead is as good as it gets when it comes to big game sportfishing, which is precisely what keeps me coming back to New York each and every fall. It should come as no surprise that I look forward to these New York trips more than any other fishing endeavors throughout the year. I just love catching big salmon and steelhead; it's that simple.

As much as I enjoy chasing kings and chrome each fall, however, there is something way more important and meaningful to pursue each and every day. Seeking a personal relationship with God through daily prayer and devotions should be our ultimate pursuit in life. There's no better way to get to know God (so far as I know) than by spending time talking with Him and studying His word. On the surface, this may not seem as fun as catching big fish, but the rewards are far more reaching. Knowing Jesus as your lord and savior is as good as it gets when it comes to earthly living, and I wouldn't trade it for all the kings and chrome in the world.

Return to the Ninemile

There is a creek in the mountains of northcentral Pennsylvania that lingers in the recesses of my outdoor memory. This creek is not very big, nor is it very deep. In fact, it is quite small, barely six feet wide at spots, and relatively shallow. It is not a particularly scenic stream as there are long sections of it that are choked with an impenetrable barrier of creekside willows. Further, it is not stocked by the Pennsylvania Fish and Boat Commission, nor is it even recognized as an approved trout water eligible for stocking. For these reasons, it is not widely known as being a good place to fish, and, for all intents and purposes, it is mostly ignored by the local angling community, which is just the way I like it.

The stream to which I am referring is Ninemile Run in Potter County. The headwaters of Ninemile Run originate from the northern slopes of the Susquehannock State Forest just west of Denton Hill State Park. From there it flows due east for approximately six miles, picking up volume from other small, mountain tributaries along its sinuous course, all the way to its confluence with the famous Pine Creek of the Pine Creek Gorge (a.k.a. the Pennsylvania Grand Canyon). Consequently, the name Ninemile Run doesn't make much sense considering that it's only about six miles long.

Despite this apparent misnomer and its other unremarkable characteristics, there is something very special about Ninemile Run. Hiding beneath its shimmering surface in numerous riffle-run complexes is an abundance of native brook trout. So many, in fact, that Ninemile Run has been designated as a Class A Wild Trout

Stream. In short, Ninemile Run doesn't need to be stocked with trout because it produces enough native/wild fish to be considered a viable sport fishery without receiving artificial implants from the state fish commission. This fantastic wild trout fishery is what makes Ninemile Run so special and why it still lingers in my outdoor memory.

The reason that Ninemile Run is but a distant memory for me is because I've only fished it once, and that was some 24 years ago. When I turned 16, my parents took me up to Potter County to do some trout fishing, and I spent two glorious days plying the Ninemile's crystal-clear waters. I have no discernible recollection of how many native brookies I caught on that trip; I just remember it being a lot, including a dandy 11-incher that I brought back home to get mounted. To this day, that trophy native brook trout (i.e., the first fish I ever had mounted) is one of the finest pieces in my ever-expanding game room collection. Much like all of my mounted animals, it serves as a physical reminder of God's awesome grace by affording me the opportunity to harvest such a magnificent creature. As such, I have looked upon this brook trout with favor many times throughout the years, thankful for having been allowed to catch it and hopeful of the opportunity to do it again someday.

For whatever reason, my return to the Ninemile took a lot longer than it should've, and on the eve of my 40th birthday I finally made it back to Potter County for the express purpose of fulfilling this longtime desire to once again fish Ninemile Run. Fortunately, the creek was much the same as I remembered it, it had changed very little during the intervening two-and-a-half decades since my last visit, and the native brook trout acted as if they hadn't seen another fisherman in all that time. They were eager to take my bait, and I was obliged to continue offering it to them one fish after another. In many respects, the fishing was even better than I remembered, and I proceeded to catch 22 trout during the first evening of my visit, including several fish in the 9 and 10-inch class.

I was having an excellent time catching these native brookies when something completely unexpected happened. The sun had already set over the western mountains, light was inevitably fading fast, and I was down to my last couple casts of the evening when a heavy fish started to tap my line. I gave him a second or two to really take the bait, and then I set the hook with a sharp jerk of the rod. The fish sprang into immediate action and made a strong run straight up the creek. I knew it was a good fish when it started to strip line from the reel, which no other fish did that entire evening. My ultralight rod was doubled over, and I started to have my doubts as to whether or not this was another brook trout. My thoughts turned to one of the wild brown trout that supposedly reside in this creek.

Earlier in the day I had been told stories by a local property owner about monster brown trout that make their way up Ninemile Run from Pine Creek. These big brownies take up residence in the deeper holes and tend to push out and/or eat all of the native brookies. He indicated that these trophy class fish are notably rare and extremely difficult to catch and that they could be in the creek for years before being caught by some unexpecting fisherman. Knowing that, the question that started to run through my mind was am I lucky enough to be that unexpecting fisherman. Unfortunately, it was too dark to see what I had hooked, but I wasn't going to take any chances and do something stupid to lose this fish. Whatever it was, I at least wanted to see it.

Sensing a perceived advantage in the fight, I gently guided the fish in my direction and then quickly pulled it up on shore. At first glance, this 17-inch wild brown trout was truly a sight to behold, and I stared in wide-eyed amazement trying to take it all in. This was an absolutely magnificent fish, a trophy catch if there ever was one. Clearly, I was not expecting, nor was I prepared, to catch a trout of this magnitude. My return to the Ninemile was intended to be singular in purpose (i.e., to catch as many native brookies as possible and have a wonderful good time in the process), and I had no earthly expectations for catching such a fish.

The gravity of the situation became increasingly more profound when I realized that this brown trout had been caught in the exact same spot as that of the 11-inch native brookie from 24 years ago. Now I was going to have two mounted fish from Ninemile Run taken from the exact same spot. Needless to say, I retired for the evening completely elated with the day's angling success. With so much to think about, it's completely understandable why I struggled to fall asleep that night. Ninemile Run was certainly proving itself to be better than I remembered or could've ever imagined, for that matter.

With the image of that big brownie still fresh in my mind, I was up at first light the next morning to see what else Ninemile Run might have in store for me. As expected, the native brookies were feeding aggressively, and I had no trouble getting into fish. I was rolling right along when I came to a moderately deep hole that was completely enclosed by overhanging willow branches. There was no way to fish this hole from a downstream approach, so I very quietly and carefully dropped in upstream and allowed my worm to slip under the tangle of branches with the rushing current. Holding the line tight against the current, I soon felt a tug on the end of my rod and proceeded to set the hook on another dandy brown trout. Once hooked, this 15-inch fish tried to make a run for deeper water, but I stopped him short and quickly pulled him out from beneath the tangle of branches. With a quick dip of the net the fight was over, and I had another trophy brownie to admire. Being two inches shorter than last night's prize catch, I decided to release this fish back into the creek to fight again another day, but not before snapping a few quick pictures for posterity. Once again, Ninemile Run had given me a magnificent fish, and I thanked God profusely for it.

I fished several more hours that morning, picking up a number of native brookies along the way, but by lunchtime I felt that I had my fill. My two-day tally stood at 41 trout, including two trophy class wild brownies. I know that I could've caught more trout if I had continued fishing, but I was content to let them be. As far as I was concerned, my return to the Ninemile was complete. The trip was an unprecedented success. No longer will Ninemile Run be a distant memory for me, nor will it take another 24 years to fish again. Streams of this nature deserve an angler's attention, and I fully intend to give it mine. Consequently, I plan to make a Potter County fishing trip an annual thing in order to ensure that Ninemile Run is no longer absent from my outdoor life.

Unfortunately, fishing in Ninemile Run wasn't the only good thing that was missing from my outdoor life for a considerable period of time. For nearly a decade, I was completely obsessed with hunting and killings things to the point that I couldn't see God's grandeur in the outdoors anymore. I was blind to God's eternal power and divine nature, which the bible tells us are clearly visible in the created world (Romans 1:20).

Even worse, I was allowing my obsession with hunting to block out the things that are truly important in life. I wasn't pursuing a deeper, personal relationship with Jesus. I wasn't spending time outdoors in God's natural creation for the purposes of experiencing His creative grandeur and drawing closer to Him in the process. I wasn't seeking the will of God to be done in my life or in the world around me for His greater glory. To the contrary, I was doing the exact opposite of these things. I was using hunting as a means of serving myself and advancing my own glory, as crazy as that may sound. In short, it was all about me and what I wanted.

It took me a long time to come to this realization, and I have sought forgiveness for it accordingly, but it does serve as a good example of how quickly our earthly desires can lead us astray. This is something that we all need to be cognizant of and actively work to keep in check. For me, it was an unhealthy passion for hunting. For others, it could be the acquisition of wealth, the advancement of a career, the development of a relationship, the pursuit of a higher social standing, etc. Anything of a worldly nature that captures our heart distracts us from our real treasure, which is Jesus.

There's no doubt that my obsession with hunting was a perversion of my love of the great outdoors, and, with God's good grace, it eventually corrected itself. Now I can fully enjoy things like fishing in Ninemile Run and other outdoor activities content in the knowledge that I am at peace in the Lord and that His goodness abounds in nature, which is precisely the way He intended it to be.

Wild on the Fly/Going Native

Trout are not like other fish. Their ornate patterns and colors, sleek streamlined design, and aggressive feeding habits put them in a class of their own. Of course, most diehard trout fishermen are quite knowledgeable of this addictive truth and spend an untold amount of time pursuing these aquatic marvels. Further, the high-gradient mountain streams and coldwater lakes that trout typically live in add even greater appeal to their overall attractiveness as a highly sought-after gamefish species. In fact, trout are so highly prized in my home state that the Pennsylvania Fish and Boat Commission expends considerable time, money, and effort stocking nearly four million of them in our lakes and streams every year just to keep anglers happy.

For as many trout fishermen as there are in Pennsylvania, there is probably an equally diverse array of methods and means for catching them. While each of these has its merits, fly fishing must surely be the most interesting and challenging. Even within the relatively small realm of fly fishing, there are dozens of different ways to go about catching trout. From high-sticking nymphs to spey-casting streamers, there is much to learn when one decides to take up fly fishing.

Fortunately, the God-given beauty of trout and the art of catching them with a fly rod have long been a part of my outdoor lifestyle. So long, in fact, that I have no discernible recollection of when or where I caught my first trout with a fly rod. It almost certainly had to be one of the stocked rainbows or brown trout in Codorus Creek (i.e., the creek that I grew up fishing), but I really can't say for sure.

That would've been sometime in the late-80's, back when Codorus Creek used to get stocked. Eventually, the Pennsylvania Fish and Boat Commission realized that they didn't need to stock Codorus Creek anymore because it supports a healthy and robust population of wild brown trout, which I have caught my fair share of over the past 20 years.

To be clear, I am not a fly fishing zealot. It is not uncommon for me to fish a section of stream with the fly rod and then turn around and fish that exact same section of stream with worms or spinners to pick up any trout that I may have missed or simply weren't interested in the fly pattern that I was using. Obviously, I only do this on those streams where it is legal to do so and when I have enough time to fish a section twice. Unfortunately, this kind of blatant malfeasance would be cited as an unpardonable blasphemy by the fly fishing elite. Consequently, I am not welcome among the ranks of the elite, which is of no substantive concern to me because I care more about catching trout than being part of some imaginary club.

However, even as a blasphemous fly fisherman, I do take it pretty seriously. I've fly fished a number of creeks throughout Pennsylvania and am not afraid to fish small, narrow creeks with lots of overhanging brush, which send many fly fishermen home in frustration. I do a lot of fly fishing in the dead of winter and have become reasonably proficient at using nymphs and streamers. I've even fly fished out west in Yellowstone country and have caught wild cutthroat trout on my own without a guide.

Despite this semi-impressive resume, though, there is still one aspect of fly fishing in which I am totally lacking. While I've managed to catch a number of trout on dry flies over the years, I've never been successful in catching a native Pennsylvania brook trout on a dry fly. This is somewhat of a mystery to me because native brook trout are supposed to be relatively easy to catch on dry flies. The fly fishing literature even goes so far as to state that "matching the hatch" is not all that important when it comes to fishing dry flies for native brookies. Any high-floating attractor pattern (i.e., stimulators, humpies, wulffs, etc.) is supposedly enough to get the job done, although I haven't found that to be the case myself.

This bothers me because I absolutely love fishing for native brook trout (i.e., the state fish of Pennsylvania) and feel that I am missing out on something special by not being able to catch them on a dry fly. To describe it more accurately, I feel incomplete as a Pennsylvania fly fisherman to have not caught a native brookie on a dry fly in nearly 30 years of fly fishing.

I could fabricate all kinds of meaningless excuses to justify why I haven't been able to catch a Keystone state native brookie on a dry fly, but they would be just that…meaningless excuses. Rather, I would prefer to spend my time and energy in the active pursuit of a remedy to this situation.

To that end, I made a personal commitment in the spring of 2017 to finally and forever rid myself of this demoralizing albatross. In short, I committed to catching a respectable (i.e., 7-inch or bigger) native brook trout on a dry fly before I did any other type of fishing, and I knew exactly which creek to use to accomplish this goal. The East Branch of the Conococheague Creek as it flows through Michaux State Forest and Caledonia State Park is my all-time favorite trout stream, and it just so happens to contain a fairly sizeable population of native brookies throughout its headwater reaches. I figured that the hemlock- and rhododendron-lined banks of this beautiful, mountain stream would make an ideal setting for such an endeavor. Therefore, the decision was made; I was going to fish the Conococheague until I caught a native brookie on a dry fly or died trying, whichever came first.

For reasons beyond my control, it took till the morning of June 3rd to find an adequate block of time in which I could go start working on this goal. I ditched the car at the lower end of Caledonia State Park and hiked a good ways down through the woods until I intercepted the creek. My plan was to steadily work my way back up the creek hitting every little nook and cranny along the way. I had three hours to fish roughly three-quarters-of-a-mile of stream. If luck was on my side, I would find at least one good native brookie that was interested in taking a dry fly somewhere in that vast stretch of water.

Starting out with a size #12 yellow stimulator, it only took about 15 minutes and 50 yards of stream to pick up my first brookie of the day. This 5-inch trout hammered the stimulator, and I had no problem setting the hook on it. While I was excited to have caught my first native brookie on a dry fly, it wasn't quite the fish I was looking for. I was hoping for something in the 7-inch range or bigger, but I was still happy to have finally caught one on a dry fly.

Continuing on, I came to a sizeable hole with a log running down through the middle of it. The water on the back side of the log looked really good, but it was going to be tough to get a fly in there without getting hung up. Switching over to a size #12 grey fox, I pulled just enough line off the reel to lay the fly about a foot beyond the log. The fly was only on the water for about a second before it was inhaled by a good fish. I set the hook immediately and did everything I could to keep the fish from getting tangled up in the log, but it dove straight for it. Miraculously, I was able to work it back out and quickly pulled it up and over the log straight into my net.

And with that, my long-time desire to catch a decent native brook trout on a dry fly was fulfilled. As I gently unhooked this 10-inch fish, I took a few seconds to admire its spectacular appearance. Native brook trout must surely be the most visually stunning fish in all of Pennsylvania. From the intricate pattern of worm-like vermiculations running down its back to its numerous red and blue-haloed side spots, the native brookie is a true sight to behold. In staring at the beauty of this fish, I was reminded why I enjoy catching them so much. And I was right, it was a special thing to catch them on a dry fly. Watching that beautiful fish come up and grab the fly off the surface was an awesome experience, and I desperately wanted to do it again.

Having another two hours left to fish, I continued on to see what else the Good Lord might have in store for me. To my surprise, I continued to hook up with trout every 15 minutes or so. While a number of them were able to wriggle free from the hook before I could get them in, I did manage to land three more brookies before it was time to go. In total, I caught five brookies and lost at least that many more. It proved to be an excellent morning on the water, and I couldn't have asked for anything more. I accomplished my goal of catching a sizeable native brookie on a dry fly (plus four more) in just under three hours of fishing on my first outing.

Given the results of this single outing, I started to question why it took so many years to accomplish this relatively easy goal. Based on what I observed that morning, it appeared that native brookies aren't that hard to catch on dry flies. In fact, my morning observations seemed to be consistent with everything that I had read about catching native brook trout on dry flies. They did, indeed, seem to be pretty willing to take flies off the surface, and they weren't real selective in the type of fly pattern. Apart from the 10-incher, which was caught on a more traditional mayfly pattern, all of the other trout were caught on a stimulator, which is nothing more than a high-floating, generic, attractor pattern. I suppose that a stimulator could be mistaken for a type of adult stonefly, but certainly none that live in the Conococheague Creek. Therefore, I came to the obvious conclusion that this three-hour outing was representative of an absolutely spectacular morning on the water that I just happened to hit at precisely the right time. If not that, then I've really been missing something for the past 30 years because it never should've taken this long to accomplish.

The only way to answer this paradoxical question was to go fishing again, so I decided to fish the exact same section of the Conococheague two weeks later. If it proved to be a bust, then I would know that my first outing was just a remarkable fluke. If, however, the results turned out to be the same, then some serious soul searching would be needed on my part. Either way, I got to go fishing again, which is never a bad thing.

If my first outing was an excellent morning on the water, my second outing proved to be even better. The water was a little lower and it was a lot more humid, but the fishing was outstanding. In just under four hours, I managed to catch ten trout on dry flies and lost at least half that many more. While four of these were stocked fish, the other six were native brookies, and they were all caught on the same size #12 stimulator that I used on my first outing.

It was a fantastic morning of fishing, and I thoroughly enjoyed every minute of it. The trout were extremely cooperative, my casting was better than normal, and I had the creek to myself. A fly fisherman couldn't ask for much more than that.

Given the results of this second outing, I now knew the answer to at least part of my question. Native brook trout are, indeed, fairly easy to catch on dry flies, but why then did it take so long to accomplish this relatively simple task? In pondering this more thoroughly, I came to the sad, but true, conclusion that it wasn't the fish that were the problem; it was me.

In looking back on my fly fishing history, I realized that the reason I never caught a native brookie on a dry fly is because I never put the effort into it. I never committed myself with any degree of thoroughness or consistency to get it done. I would use dry flies until I got frustrated or tangled up in the brush and then switch over to nymphs or streamers. Had I been more patient and stuck with it, the results would've surely been different and it never would've taken so long to accomplish this fairly easy task. I simply didn't put the necessary effort into it, and that's all there is to it.

Obviously, this same concept applies to a lot of things in life, including getting to know God. Getting to know God does not come without putting some effort into it. Jesus is standing at the door of our heart knocking, but we need to do more than just open the door. Opening the door is just the beginning. Once we've opened that door, we need to commit ourselves with the appropriate level of effort to get to know Him. We need to spend time studying His word, meditating on its meaning. We need to attend church where we can learn about God and godly living in a group setting with a body of fellow believers. And, perhaps most importantly, we need to talk with Him through daily prayer and devotions.

Fortunately, none of these things are particularly difficult, but they do require a certain degree of effort on our part. If we commit to expending this effort, with any degree of thoroughness or consistency, the results will be rewarding beyond measure. After all, getting to know God is the single greatest thing that we can ever hope to accomplish during our time on this earth. It's even better than catching a native brook trout on a dry fly, and that takes some people upwards of 30 years to accomplish!

The Grand Deception

There's no such thing as an honest fisherman. Each and every one of us that takes to the water with rod in hand does so with the intentions of trickery and deceit. Even the good fishermen are untrustworthy, as their success is little more than a measure of their ability to be deceptive. Truly I tell you, there's not an honest one among us.

This may seem a little odd at first, but the more you think about it, the more you'll come to realize that I'm right. Fishing, more so than any other recreational activity on the planet, relies entirely on the ability of its participant to be cunning and deceitful. Some would argue that hunting also requires a fair amount of deception on the part of its participant, and if we were talking about waterfowl or spring gobbler hunting, I would generally agree with that assertion. However, I've shot a number of deer over the years that were the simple result of being at the right place at the right time. There was no illicit deception required on my part whatsoever. Conversely, I cannot say the same about fishing.

At its core, fishing involves nothing more than a fisherman using trickery and deceit to con some unsuspecting fish into biting his line. And the lengths to which some fishermen go to make that happen are unparalleled in the modern world. From the use of ultra-low visibility fluorocarbon line to real-image photographic imprinted lures, fishermen will stop at nothing to fool their intended quarry. Even bait fishermen are harbingers of deceit because they go about offering their various delectables as if they were a natural occurrence (i.e., manna from heaven) that just so happens to fall from the sky and land in the water at that precise location. Little do the fish know that there is a sharp and stinging reality awaiting them.

Ultimately, it's the presentation of a lure or bait that is responsible for initiating this grand deception, but there's a whole suite of specialized gear and equipment that goes into it. Beyond the basics of hook, line, and sinker, fishermen employ a mindboggling array of supplementary items to aid in their fraudulent enterprise, up to and including aerodynamically designed speedboats that are fully equipped with all the latest electronic gadgetry.

Vast sums of money can be spent in a very short timeframe trying to outfit oneself for the purposes of launching a wide-ranging assault (i.e., a pre-emptive strike) on the aquatic environment and, in particular, its finned inhabitants. In that regard, most serious fishermen are well-equipped, patient, and calculating. They know that it's just a matter of time for their devious ploy to prove effective.

As for me, I'm just as guilty in my angling transgressions as every other fisherman out there. I use a tremendous diversity of lures and baits at various times and locations for the purposes of fooling multiple species of fish into biting my line. Further, I have an extensive array of different rods and reels with which to wield these various lures and baits. From ultralight trout rods to heavy duty surf fishing outfits, I am equipped to do battle with almost every kind of fish known to man.

Beyond these fundamental elements, nothing else is needed to be an effective fish deceiver, but I have a secret weapon that really stacks the deck in my favor. Several years ago, I bought a kayak, and it has revolutionized a significant component of my fishing program.

Lake and river fishing will never be the same for me again as a result of the increased mobility that comes by way of the kayak. I can go just about anywhere I want, and it's super quiet. For all intents and purposes, kayak fishing can be characterized as operating in stealth mode. It's low profile fishing at its best, and it's extremely effective.

If I had known how effective fishing from a kayak can be, I would've bought one years ago. Ironically, I didn't even buy my kayak for fishing purposes. I bought it to go birding on some of the lakes and rivers of the Adirondack Mountains of New York. It was only by chance that I discovered its lethal effectiveness for fishing.

While up in the Adirondacks, I took the kayak out fishing one evening and ended up catching a 40-inch, trophy-class northern pike on my first time out. In the days that followed, I caught several more pike, a small muskie, and more than a dozen largemouth bass all while using the kayak. This was an eye-opening experience, and I was not ignorant of its significance. I was keenly aware of its lethal prowess. While it was originally designated for bird watching, I was quick to repurpose it for fishing endeavors.

Upon returning home from New York, I visited several lakes and streams in Pennsylvania with the kayak to continue my assessment of its angling effectiveness. From smallmouths in the Conodoguinet Creek to perch at Locust Lake, I continued to be highly impressed with the fish-catching results. The stealth and subterfuge that come part and parcel with kayak fishing are unbeatable, and I have since mounted two permanent rod holders on the front of my kayak, thereby cementing its place in my arsenal of must-have fishing equipment.

Two fish that I particularly enjoy catching when fishing from the kayak are the northern pike and the chain pickerel.

These long, slender, toothy critters are apex predators that aggressively attack their prey. They lurk in the shadows (i.e., underneath docks, in weed beds, among lily pads, etc.) waiting for unsuspecting baitfish to venture close, and then they strike with deadly speed and accuracy. In short, they ambush their prey; it's what pike and pickerel are known for.

The primary technique that I use to trick these aggressive predators into striking is ripping a stick bait. The jerking and erratic action that is created by ripping a stick bait is deadly on pike and pickerel. It triggers their predatory instinct, and the resulting strikes tend to be vicious. As a result, there's no mistaking it when a pike or pickerel hits a stick bait. That's why I like catching them so much, especially when using the kayak.

Unfortunately, I don't have a lot of options for catching pike in close proximity to my southcentral Pennsylvania residence. There's only one lake in my neck of the woods that has pike in it (that I know of), and that lake is significantly overfished. Consequently, the pike are exceptionally wary and hard to catch in this lake, and I don't often fish it because of that.

Instead, I rely on my annual New York salmon fishing trips to get my fill of pike fishing. The estuary of the Salmon River, which is easily accessible via kayak, contains extensive weed beds that harbor a fair number of northern pike, and I use my downtime between morning and evening salmon fishing sessions to throw stick baits for hungry pike.

I first discovered this northern pike fishery several years ago purely by accident. While using the kayak to troll stick baits through the estuary for salmon, I accidentally caught a nice pike. This was a revealing discovery, and I have since caught a number of pike (intentionally) in the Salmon River estuary while fishing from the kayak. None of these Salmon River pike, to date, have been as big as that initial 40-incher from the Adirondacks, but they are still really fun to catch in the kayak and they provide some great angling action when the salmon fishing is at its lowest.

While I generally rely on the state of New York to meet my pike fishing needs, I don't have to go as far to get the same for chain pickerel. Laurel Lake in Pine Grove Furnace State Park, which is less than 20 miles from my house, contains a viable population of chain pickerel. Using the kayak early in the morning or late in the evening to probe the lily pads and shoreline structure of this 25-acre impoundment is a surefire way to fool some aggressive pickerel into hitting a stick bait. While they aren't as big as pike, pickerel can be just as aggressive, and they're a real treat to catch when kayak fishing.

Prior to my acquisition of the kayak, I had never caught a pickerel at Laurel Lake. However, with the newly discovered stealth and mobility of this secret weapon, it's become a regular thing to catch at least one pickerel on every outing, and I have since come to expect it. This heightened expectation simply wouldn't be possible without the kayak. I just wish I would've discovered this secret weapon years ago; there's no telling how many more fish I could've conned into biting my line.

All kidding aside, it's important to recognize and be fully cognizant of the fact that we live in a world where trickery and deceit are waiting at our doorstep ready to pounce at every opportunity, and I'm not talking about the innocent kind of trickery and deceit associated with fishing. Satan has riddled the world with all manner of lies, tricks, distractions, and deceptions in a concerted and calculated effort to lure us away from God. He doesn't want us to know and follow God because that would go against his treacherous plan for humanity, and he will stop at nothing to bring us down. This is and always has been Satan's devious ploy – the grand deception of the world. We need to look no further than the temptation of Adam and Eve in the Garden of Eden to see how Satan works.

However, the good thing about all of this is that we can have full assurance and confidence in God because He is infinitely bigger, stronger, and better than the deceiver. Where Satan is cunning, God is loving. Where Satan spreads lies and misconceptions, God speaks the righteous truth. Where Satan attempts to deceive and destroy, God saves and redeems. In fact, God loves us so much that He created us in His own image and then gave us free will to make our own decisions in life. We are not commanded or coerced into loving and following God. We have the God-given ability to choose for ourselves what path we take in life. We can elect to take on God and godly living, or we can go a different way. The choice is ours, but the end results are vastly different.

As for me and my house, we will not be victims of deception, but rather, we will choose the Lord and walk in faith with Jesus, the god of truth and life.

Avifaunal Outings

A Golden Day

All night long I could hear the wind lashing against the side of the house. It was the type of wind that rattles the siding and makes the aluminum downspouts vibrate in a low harmonic tune. I tried to block it out as best I could, but the wind was relentless. Suffice it to say, sleep did not come easy.

The cause of all this wind, and my subsequent lack of sleep, was an arctic cold front that had pushed south out of Canada, crossed the Great Plains – dumping nearly a foot of snow in the mid-west, and was now roaring its way east through the mid-Atlantic region right past my southcentral Pennsylvania residence. The weatherman warned that this cold front was coming and that it would be followed by steady northwest winds and cold arctic air. As I drew the covers a little tighter around my shoulders, my thoughts instinctively turned to the Kittatinny Ridge, which is situated just a few miles north of my house, and the untold number of golden eagles that it would see today as a result of this passing cold front.

It was the 8th of November, and this was just the type of weather system that I was hoping for. Early to mid-November is primetime for golden eagle migration here in Pennsylvania, and every raptor enthusiast yearns for a migration-spurring cold front, like the one that kept me up all night, to move through at this precise time of year. Such cold fronts and the northwest winds that accompany them create the necessary thermals and updrafts that can result in big pushes of golden eagles within a relatively short timeframe. Lucky is the birder who capitalizes on these special opportunities.

Recognizing the day's potential, I planned to spend at least part of it up at the Waggoner's Gap Hawk Watch, my local hawk watching destination of choice. Located just north of Carlisle on the crest of the Kittatinny Ridge, the Waggoner's Gap Hawk Watch provides a front row seat to the autumn raptor migration. This is the same spot that two months ago I enjoyed watching broad-winged and sharp-shined hawks pour down the ridge in what appeared to be a seemingly endless parade of birds. With these birds long gone, it was now time for the peak of the golden eagle migration.

There are several other established hawk watching destinations along the Kittatinny Ridge here in Pennsylvania, including the famous Hawk Mountain Sanctuary, but Waggoner's Gap is the closest to my house and it tends to be less crowded than some of the more well-known sites. Therefore, it's my "go to" spot for watching the autumn raptor flight.

To those who have no interest in bird watching, the concept of sitting on a windswept ridge in the middle of November is not terribly appealing. However, I would venture to say that those who feel this way have probably never had the experience of watching a golden eagle come floating down the ridge, passing directly over their head, without ever flapping its wings even once. It's an experience that leaves some people speechless the first time it happens, and one that never grows old or loses its awe-inspiring effect regardless of how many times a person witnesses it.

Unfortunately, due to some unavoidable work obligations, I didn't make it up to Waggoner's Gap until 1:00 P.M., but I quickly settled in among the other observers and got ready for whatever the wind would blow our way. Watching the northeastern skyline, it first appeared as a distant speck, a tiny anomaly in the relatively uniform background of the gray cloud cover. With the aid of my 12-power binoculars, I could see that it was a bird, a raptor for sure, but it was too far away to render any sort of positive identification.

Catching an updraft like an aerodynamic surfer, it circled high into the air and then pitched southward straight down the ridge. Moving at a high rate of speed, it quickly closed the gap between us, and I could now see that it was indeed a golden eagle. With its long, steady wings locked into soaring position, it passed by just to our left, no more than 200 feet above the crest of the ridge, and disappeared into the unknown. It was a remarkable experience, and I felt a bit awestruck by the whole thing. I had been there for less than thirty minutes and already had the quintessential golden eagle migration experience. Little did I know that this was the 12th golden eagle of the day and that there would be six more experiences just like it before the day drew to a close.

Coming down off the ridge at dusk, I was mesmerized by the seven golden eagles that I had just seen. Totaling eighteen for the day, it ranked as one of the best golden eagle migration days in modern history at the Waggoner's Gap Hawk Watch. While I would've liked to have been there for the entire show, I'm just glad that I was able to ditch work and catch the majority of the afternoon flight. It was a day that I won't soon forget – a golden day if there ever was one.

It goes without saying that a spectacular day outdoors like this serves to remind me just how much I enjoy and appreciate God's natural creation, but it also reminds me of the fact that there is a much greater day still to come. As the bible tells us, one day Jesus will return in power and glory to rightfully claim the earth as His kingdom. He will take His place on an earthly throne and set things straight in this broken world. He will make all things new and righteous again. Nobody knows when this will happen, but the bible guarantees that it will indeed happen. In the interim, we are to be prepared and keep an ever-watchful eye for the return of the Lord. Now that will be a true golden day like no other.

On the Rocks

I'll be the first to admit that I'm not a big fan of the beach. I can generally make do and be content just about anywhere, but, for various and sundry reasons, the beach has just never really been my thing. It's not that I have anything against it; I'm just not much of a beach person.

First and foremost of my reasons for not being a big beach person is the simple fact that it's not the mountains. For as long as I can remember, I've always preferred to spend my time in the mountains, among the forested ridges and secluded hollows, of my home state of Pennsylvania as opposed to the coarse-sand beaches of the nearby mid-Atlantic coast. Generally speaking, there is a lot more for a person like me to do in the mountains than at the beach. With all the hunting, fishing, hiking, camping, and bird watching that can be done in the mountains, it's no wonder why I prefer them over the beach.

Second, I don't particularly care for being hot, sticky, and sandy, which is the normal outcome of my summertime beach experiences. There's no doubt that taking a dip in the ocean can be refreshing on a hot, summer day, but the sun-scorching agony, sandy drawers, and overall grimy feeling that typically accompany these brief respites are generally not worth it. Besides, I can think of at least a dozen different ways that I would prefer to cool off on a hot, summer day than swimming in the salty ocean.

Finally, and perhaps most importantly, I have no interest in the crowds of people or the types of recreational activities that are typically associated with the beach. From jet skiing to skimboarding, I've never been terribly excited about the great volume of people or the types of activities that they normally engage in while spending time at the beach. Again, I'm just not much of a beach person, and that's all there is to it.

Despite my rather lackluster opinion of the beach, there is one aspect of this coastal environment that I do thoroughly enjoy, but only on a seasonal basis. The wintertime bird watching along the mid-Atlantic coast can be downright spectacular, and I try to hit the beach at least once every winter to take in the show.

There's no doubt about it, the beach was made for wintertime bird watching. Gone are the hordes of half-baked sunbathers, the raucous jet skiers, and the thrill-seeking parasailers that besiege this place, en masse, during the summer vacation season. In their place are scores of majestic sea ducks, flocks of overwintering shorebirds, legions of different gulls and terns, and even the occasional pelagic species. For all intents and purposes, the beaches, inlets, and bays are left to the birds and those hearty souls who enjoy looking at them, which is precisely why I like to visit the beach at this time of year.

Standing on the rocks of Ocean City's North Jetty or along the boulder-lined Indian River Inlet just a few miles north in Delaware, one can see large rafts of sea ducks, including black, surf, and white-winged scoters, long-tailed ducks, and common eiders that have moved south for the winter in search of more readily available food supplies. With a careful eye, one may even be able to spot a rare harlequin duck, which are known to frequent these rocky protrusions during the winter months. Lucky, indeed, is the birder who gets to see a drake harlequin diving along the rock jetties of the mid-Atlantic coast.

Also quite common at this time of year are overwintering loons of both the common and red-throated varieties. It's not unusual to see them disappear under the water only to resurface some distance away with a fresh catch dangling between their bills. In regard to piscivorous water birds, it should also be noted that red-breasted mergansers, buffleheads, horned grebes, double-crested cormorants, and great cormorants can be seen with relative ease from these rocky vantage points during the winter months.

Speaking of rocky vantage points, these tend to be the haunts of mixed flocks of purple sandpipers and ruddy turnstones, which always seem to be present along the rock jetties in winter. On more than one occasion, I've had purple sandpipers and ruddy turnstones feeding on the exposed mussels along the lower boulders within a few feet of me. I've also had the privilege of seeing dunlins, sanderlings, oystercatchers, brant, and a lost red knot along these rocks at various times throughout the winter months.

If the sea ducks, loons, and shorebirds aren't enough to satisfy, one could easily spend several hours studying the various gulls and terns that are always flying about. Great black-backed gulls, herring gulls, ring-billed gulls, Bonaparte's gulls, common terns, and Forster's terns of numerous age-classes are readily available for inspection. In fact, the Ocean City Inlet parking lot is a great place to find most of these species, where one can approach to within a few feet without causing much of a stir. While this is certainly not encouraged, the acquisition of a fresh batch of boardwalk fries will attract as many gulls as one cares to see at an extremely close range. Less accommodating species, such as Bonaparte's gulls and Forster's terns, are best viewed by watching the turbulent waters of the inlets.

And, of course, who could forget the pelagics – the rare alcids (i.e., razorbills and dovekies) and gannets – that can occasionally be seen from these inlet locations. While it's only happened for me once, I will never forget that cold, February morning when two razorbills came floating into the Indian River Inlet and started diving for food right in front of me. It was a magical thing, something that I had long been hoping for, and I thoroughly enjoyed every minute of it.

Similarly, I will never forget the December morning that I happened upon three northern gannets peacefully resting on the water at the tip of the North Jetty in Ocean City. Prior to spreading their enormous wings and gracefully lifting into the air, I was afforded a few precious seconds in which to inspect their finer details at an extremely close range. I had seen gannets here before, but never resting on the water like this. All my previous gannet sightings were of birds soaring over the open water or diving into the ocean far offshore. Seeing these normally pelagic species so close to shore and peacefully resting on the water was a special treat and made for quite an exciting morning.

Considering all the potential species that could be encountered on any winter day, birding at the Ocean City Inlet, in combination with the nearby Indian River Inlet, can be a pretty amazing experience. Add in the coastal bays, tidal salt marshes, bayberry thickets, maritime forests, and freshwater ponds that surround these areas, and the total number of potential species increases exponentially. Suffice it to say, tolerating the wind and cold to see this great diversity of species seems like a small price to pay for such an excellent show. After all, when it comes to coastal birding, that's what being on the rocks is all about.

Unfortunately, as good as the coastal birding is during the winter months, I was slow to recognize it. Due to my self-ascribed aversion to the beach, I did my best to avoid it for a considerable period of time. I wasn't even giving it a chance to find out if there might be something positive about it. As a result, I missed out on some fantastic birding opportunities that I could've been taking advantage of.

In much the same way, I fear that a lot of people shy away from God and godly living because they don't think it has anything positive to offer. All they see are a bunch of rules and nonsensical "rituals" that have no meaning or value. When considering the Christian lifestyle, some people even see it as being too limiting on their personal freedom and don't want to have anything to do with it.

In reality, nothing could be further from the truth. Getting to know God and choosing to walk in faith with Jesus brings total satisfaction and ultimate freedom to one's life. There is absolutely nothing negative or even remotely limiting about it. Wanting to please God by following His commandments is a natural progression of Christian growth and comes part and parcel with a deeper, more meaningful, spiritually rewarding, and emotionally fulfilling life. Unfortunately, by not giving God a chance, many people have no idea what they're missing, and the ramifications are far worse than being a little late to a good birding show. These folks are really on the rocks and not in a good way.

If you've been slow or unwilling to follow God and take on a godly life, I urge you to reconsider. You might just be surprised at how awesome it is.

Oddballs

Birders are a strange lot, and those of us who are passionate about our bird watching endeavors would probably agree with this to some extent. Generally speaking, we tend to do things that most folks find to be somewhat odd. From keeping a detailed life list with specific dates and locations of sightings to conducting a physically exhausting and financially draining big year, birders are, admittedly, just a little off when compared to the norms of mainstream society. It's okay, though, because most of us birders so enjoy God's winged creatures that we have no great desire or care to be compared to these so-called "norms" of society. Such inconsequential judgements are of no concern to us, and we are quite content to go on enjoying our avifaunal fixations one bird at a time regardless of what others may think about us.

As strange as us birders may be, however, sometimes the birds act even more strange. Consider, for example, the late-April day several years ago when I and a group of fellow birders watched an American golden-plover and a ruff feeding in a flooded field just outside the small town of Snow Hill, Maryland. We all stared in wide-eyed amazement and disbelief at these birds because we knew that the golden-plover was on the wrong side of the continent and that the ruff was on the wrong side of the world. How these oddball birds ended up in a flooded field in Worcester County, Maryland was more than any of us could explain. It sure did make for an exciting morning of birding though.

Oddball bird sightings such as this are not particularly rare. There always seems to be something amiss in the bird world, some strange anomaly, that keeps us birders on the go. Such oddball sightings are every bit as exciting as they are strange, and birders rush to take advantage of these life list-bolstering opportunities before they disappear.

In most instances, the cause or reason for these aberrant sightings is largely speculative. Sometimes birds get blown off course by powerful storm systems that push them hundreds of miles outside their normal range. In other cases, migrating birds simply miss their mark or take a turn in the wrong direction and end up a long way off from where they're supposed to be. Some may be escaped pets or caged releases (like the chukar that I discovered near my southcentral Pennsylvania home a couple years ago) that are just trying to find their way in an unfamiliar natural environment. These are logical and rational explanations for some oddball bird sightings, but others are simply inexplicable.

The following accounts are just a couple examples of the oddball bird sightings that I've been treated to over the years. In each of these examples, the subject bird was observed well outside of its known range for no readily apparent reason. Despite the rather mysterious circumstances of these sightings, each one was considered to be a rare and special gift that will likely never happen again, and I count myself fortunate to have been so blessed.

Cumberland Valley Prairie Falcon:

The Cumberland Valley in southcentral Pennsylvania occupies the large swath of land between the northern tip of the Blue Ridge Mountains and the Kittatinny Ridge of the undulating Ridge and Valley Physiographic Province. Given its unique topographic and geographic location, the

Cumberland Valley is no stranger to oddball bird sightings. One of its strangest, however, was a reoccurring prairie falcon for eight consecutive winters between 2005 and 2012.

As its name implies, the prairie falcon is a bird of western rangelands that is rarely spotted east of the Mississippi River. According to the rare bird sighting statistics maintained by the Pennsylvania Ornithological Records Committee (PORC), this reoccurring individual is the only prairie falcon to ever be recorded in Pennsylvania. Needless to say, the origin of this bird was the topic of much discussion and debate, but it was eventually accepted by PORC as a confirmed Pennsylvania occurrence.

Given the unique status of this bird, I made the drive over to the Cumberland Valley to see this falcon on several occasions throughout the years. Each time I saw it, I felt a tingle of excitement because I knew I was looking at something special. Nobody knows whatever became of this prairie falcon, nor does anyone know where it ever came from, but a great many mid-Atlantic birders were able to add prairie falcon to their life list because of this reoccurring individual.

Eastern Shore Scissor-tailed Flycatcher:

October is a magical time on the Eastern Shore of Virginia. This long, slender peninsula between the Chesapeake Bay and the Atlantic Ocean provides a natural migration corridor for an untold number of raptors, shorebirds, and songbirds. With its diverse mix of open water habitats, sand beaches, tidal salt marshes, exposed mudflats, agricultural fields, and maritime forests, it's quite possible to tally more than a hundred species in a single day during the peak of the autumn migration.

One species that you should not plan on seeing on the Eastern Shore of Virginia, though, is the scissor-tailed flycatcher. For all intents and purposes, the scissor-tailed flycatcher is a bird of the open grasslands of Texas, Oklahoma, and Nebraska, not the Eastern Shore of Virginia. Nonetheless, that's exactly where I saw my life list scissor-tailed flycatcher.

While participating in the annual Eastern Shore of Virginia Birding and Wildlife Festival, we got word that a juvenile scissor-tailed flycatcher had been spotted in an overgrown apple tree just a couple miles from where we were. Not wanting to miss this potential life list species, we high-tailed it over to the reported spot and quickly found the bird perched amongst the dense tangle of branches. It didn't appear to be hurt or injured in any way; it was just peacefully enjoying the afternoon. Admittedly, there was a major tropical storm hanging just off the coast of Virginia at that time, but none of the other birders I talked to felt that was the cause of this oddball sighting. It was just another crazy case of a bird going rogue.

Mid-Atlantic Pacific Loon:

There's no place I'd rather be on a cold, winter day than Ocean City, Maryland. This may seem like an odd time of year to visit a beach-resort destination like Ocean City, but anyone who thinks that must not be aware of how good the coastal birding is. Winter at the Ocean City Inlet is a great time of year to spot gannets, harlequins, eiders, scoters, long-tailed ducks, buffleheads, red-breasted mergansers, brant, horned grebes, common and red-throated loons, purple sandpipers, ruddy turnstones, and even the occasional razorbill. On any given winter day, the Ocean City Inlet and surrounding coastal bays can make for an excellent birding experience, and I try to hit it at least once every year to enjoy the show.

Of all my mid-winter birding trips to Ocean City, February 16, 2013 stands out as one to remember. For obvious reasons, Pacific loons are not a bird that I expect to see along Maryland's mid-Atlantic coast, but that's exactly what we found there on that cold, February morning. Diving among the common and red-throated loons was a single Pacific loon. Having already seen a Pacific loon up in Alaska, I wasn't able to add this western anomaly as a new life list species, but it sure did make for an interesting morning of bird watching at the Ocean City Inlet. Who knows if another Pacific loon will ever be spotted at this location again?

Conodoguinet Creek Western Grebe:

The Conodoguinet Creek is a large stream that lazily meanders its way across Cumberland County in southcentral Pennsylvania. It's a direct tributary to the mighty Susquehanna River just across from the state capital of Harrisburg. It's a stream of deep holes and big oxbows that are rich in aquatic life. Not surprisingly, it's also a stream of migrating waterfowl, nesting bald eagles, and scores of great blue herons. As a result, the Conodoguinet is a great creek for bird watching.

Despite its birdy nature, the Conodoguinet is not a place to go looking for western grebes, but that's exactly what a couple birders found there back in February of 2009. Similar to the Pacific loon noted above, western grebes did not get their name by hanging out along the eastern seaboard. In fact, the Pennsylvania Ornithological Records Committee eventually confirmed that this was the first official sighting of a western grebe in Pennsylvania. Consequently, this bird attracted a lot of attention from the local birding community, and I didn't waste any time in making a visit to the Conodoguinet to see it for myself.

I'm glad I did because it only stuck around for a couple days before disappearing into the wild blue yonder. This western grebe was only in Pennsylvania for a short time, but it sure did cause quite a stir while it was here. Given its geographic location and the time of year in which it was spotted in Pennsylvania, this western grebe was another inexplicable oddity that seemed to defy all logical explanation.

Mispillion Harbor King Eider:

The Dupont Nature Center at the Mispillion Harbor Reserve, where the Mispillion River meets the Delaware Bay in Kent County, Delaware, is a well-known spot to witness the great spectacle of nature that involves thousands of migrating shorebirds ravenously feeding on the freshly laid eggs of Atlantic horseshoe crabs. The relationship between migrating shorebirds (i.e., red knots, semipalmated sandpipers, and ruddy turnstones) and breeding horseshoe crabs is a natural phenomenon that has garnered the Delaware Bay ecosystem international recognition for its avian importance. As a result, the back porch of the Dupont Nature Center can get a bit crowded with eager bird watchers during the peak of the spring shorebird migration.

While many birds are seasonal visitors at the Mispillion Harbor Reserve, one in particular stands out. In August of 2013, a lone king eider showed up out of nowhere. It's not unusual for common eiders to move south along the Atlantic Coast during the winter months, but it is highly abnormal for a king eider to do that, especially in summer. Needless to say, the back porch of the Dupont Nature Center saw a lot of action when this oddball eider showed up.

Fortunately, I had plans to be in Delaware for other matters at this exact time, and a quick trip over to the Dupont Nature Center was all that was needed to see this new life list species. This juvenile male eider seemed oddly out of place, but notably content floating around the tidal waters of the Mispillion Harbor. What caused this lone eider to fly south in summer is a mystery that will likely never be solved, but I'm sure glad that he did. From what I could tell, I think a lot of other mid-Atlantic birders were pretty excited about it too.

Berks County Black-backed Oriole:

Of all my oddball bird sightings, the Berks County black-backed oriole is, by far, the strangest. Black-backed orioles are endemic to the subtropical highland forests of central Mexico, where they thrive on a predominantly insectivorous diet. However, that didn't stop one from spending the winter of 2017 in southeast Pennsylvania.

On January 31st, a resident of a small housing development in Lower Heidelberg Township in Berks County, Pennsylvania reported seeing a strange oriole in his yard. A picture of the bird was posted on Facebook, where it was positively identified as a black-backed oriole.

From that point on, chaos erupted in the world of bird watching. Birders from across the country flocked to Pennsylvania to get a look at this rare bird, which was very accommodating for the crowds of anxious onlookers as it fed on the grapes and orange slices that had been put out for it. Two weeks later, when I finally got around to making a visit to Berks County to have a look at this strange oriole, there had already been upwards of 1,400 people who signed the visitors log. To say that this bird caused a stir would be a bit of an understatement. Birders came from as far away as California, Texas, Arizona, and Ontario to get a look at this anomaly.

A black-backed oriole was spotted in San Diego, California back in 2000, but that bird was eventually dismissed as being an escaped pet. If this Berks County bird is eventually confirmed by the Pennsylvania Ornithological Records Committee and accepted by the American Birding Association as being a legitimate occurrence, it will be the first official record of a black-backed oriole in the United States. Hence the reason that this bird caused a near-panic among the more high-strung members of the bird watching community. I guess we'll just have to wait and see what the professionals decide to do with the recordation of this species. Given the complexities associated with making such a determination, it will likely take a couple years before any formal decision is rendered. Until that time comes, many hardcore life listers will be on pins and needles hoping for a positive result. As for me, I'm counting it either way and have already made an entry for it in my personal life list.

While these are just a couple examples of the oddball bird sightings that I've been treated to over the years, they do show the highly variable nature of such occurrences. To put it quite simply, an oddball bird sighting can involve just about any species at any location at any time of year. Needless to say, such occurrences keep us birders on the go and make for some really exciting times afield.

Beyond making for some exciting times afield, oddball bird sightings serve to remind me of two fundamental biblical truths. The first of these deals with the futility of worrying about yourself and your various life circumstances. In Matthew 6:26, Jesus tells us that God takes care of the birds of the air, even the poor lost ones, and then invites us to consider how much more our heavenly father will take care of us. In so doing, Jesus is essentially saying that there's no need to worry about things because God, who loves us and cares for us, is always looking out for us. Just as God will look after and care for the poor bird that went astray, He will do the same, if not considerably more, for us too. This is a very reassuring concept because we live in a world where there are no guarantees in life and anything can happen at any time. It certainly is comforting to know that God, the ruler and maker of all things, has our back.

The second biblical truth that oddball bird sightings tend to remind me of is the fact that God will always welcome us back home when we tend to go astray in life. This was highlighted in Luke 15:11-32, where Jesus tells us a story about a wayward son that squanders his early inheritance and then comes crawling back home to his father looking for help. In the Parable of the Prodigal Son, Jesus explains that the father (who is God) joyfully accepts the wayward son (who is us) and celebrates his return home regardless of what he has done. Again, it's comforting to know that when we go astray in life, as we and birds sometimes do, God will always be there waiting for us and welcome us back home with open arms.

Both of these biblical truths are important for us to know and remember. They speak to the loving nature of God and how wonderful He really is. It seems only fitting that a part of His miraculous creation, however lost or out of place they may be, should serve to remind us of these things.

Getting Paid for It

Getting paid to do something that you thoroughly enjoy and would otherwise do for free is a pretty sweet deal, especially when it involves your full-time, permanent job. Beyond the obvious financial benefit that comes from getting paid, the opportunity to do something that you truly enjoy at a professional level can be a very rewarding experience. In most instances, it takes the activity to a whole new level and allows you to go beyond the ordinary. Sometimes it even involves doing certain things or getting access to certain places that you otherwise wouldn't be able to do or see, respectively. This makes it really exciting because these kinds of opportunities probably wouldn't come about if they weren't part of a paid work assignment.

Now, just imagine that these paid work assignments are entirely and purposely related to some aspect of bird watching. As hard as that may be to imagine, it does apply, at least in part, to what I do for a living. As a professional environmental scientist at an engineering-environmental consulting firm, I am occasionally tasked with a field assignment that leaves me shaking my head in disbelief that someone is actually willing to pay me to do this. Such field assignments are notably rare and highly coveted by my fellow coworkers, but they do come my way from time to time.

Typically, these field assignments are related to some imperiled species that is listed at either the state or federal level as being threatened or endangered, which is precisely why we do a lot of work related to bog turtles and Indiana bats. However, we do get bird-related assignments every now and again, and they usually get sent my way because I'm the designated "bird guy" at our firm.

Over the years, these assignments have involved such things as monitoring a great blue heron rookery, conducting a prothonotary warbler survey, leading a winter waterfowl survey, conducting comprehensive breeding bird surveys, and monitoring active bald eagle and peregrine falcon nest sites. For each of these assignments, I was tasked with completing the necessary field work in accordance with whatever methods and means I felt to be appropriate to get the job done. This could entail anything from just a few hours of targeted field work up to and including multi-day endeavors to ensure survey effectiveness. On a couple occasions, it even required the use of a boat to survey relatively inaccessible portions of a river. In all instances, it was a spectacular time afield getting paid to do something that was really fun.

Perhaps, one of the most interesting and challenging bird-related assignments that I've had, however, was the charge to get certified as a FIDS observer in the state of Maryland. As part of the regulatory requirements associated with Maryland's Chesapeake Bay Critical Area Program, large tracts of contiguous forestland that are known to support a breeding population of forest interior dwelling species (or FIDS) are protected from development.

Generally speaking, FIDS include various warblers, thrushes, vireos, and tanagers, as well as several other woodland species that need large tracts on unbroken forest habitat for breeding purposes. Such species as the cerulean warbler, Louisiana waterthrush, yellow-throated vireo, scarlet tanager, wood thrush, pileated woodpecker, barred owl, and whip-poor-will are classic FIDS.

Once a particular tract of forestland is determined to be FIDS habitat, any encroachment into it or forest clearing activities must be mitigated by permanently preserving other known FIDS habitat or by creating adequate replacement FIDS habitat at another location. Obviously, most developers aren't too fond of the requirement to mitigate for their forestland impacts by providing adequate replacement land, so there is a notable financial benefit to having their particular tract of forestland determined to not be FIDS habitat.

That's where a certified FIDS observer comes in. A developer can hire a certified FIDS observer to conduct a mandatory three-day survey of the particular woodlot to determine if it supports any breeding FIDS. Naturally, these surveys need to be conducted during the peak of the breeding season for neotropical migrants, which generally corresponds to the month of June.

As such, there is a definite potential for paid FIDS work in the state of Maryland, which is precisely why my boss wanted to get someone on the list of certified observers. Without being on the list, there is no opportunity for our firm to conduct this kind of work. This is where I come in. Being the designated "bird guy", I was charged with doing whatever it takes to get certified as a FIDS observer, so that we have someone on the list.

As one might expect, getting certified as a FIDS observer is not as easy as making a phone call or writing a request letter. It requires a one-on-one field examination with the State Zoologist from the Maryland Department of Natural Resources (DNR). Further, since FIDS surveys are conducted during the month of June after full leaf-out conditions, they are primarily auditory in nature and require the observer to be able to identify multiple species entirely by ear and ear alone. This takes birding to a whole new level when you have to be able to identify every species you encounter just by hearing its song without even seeing the bird.

Consequently, I needed to do some practicing to brush up on my bird songs prior to my June 19th field exam. To that end, I spent several mornings in the local state forest during the first two weeks of June relearning my forest interior bird songs. At the end of these practice sessions, I was feeling pretty confident with my auditory bird identification skills and could positively identify just about every bird I was hearing.

On the morning of the 19th, I awoke at 3:30 A.M. and made the two-hour drive to the designated meeting spot off I-68 in the mountains of western Maryland. The plan for my FIDS observer test was to meet up with the State Zoologist at 6:00 A.M. and spend the next several hours conducting independent point counts at various locations throughout the Sideling Hill Wildlife Management Area and Green Ridge State Forest. To pass the test, I needed the results of my point counts to be within 85% of the State Zoologist's; a daunting task, indeed, considering that this was being done entirely by ear at two places I've never been to before. At least I could take some degree of solace in knowing that I was getting paid to go birding even if I didn't pass the test, although the boss would probably have something negative to say about that.

Starting out at the Sideling Hill Wildlife Management Area, we were quick to find indigo bunting, red-eyed vireo, yellow-throated vireo, scarlet tanager, worm-eating warbler, northern parula, ovenbird, wood thrush, white-breasted nuthatch, tufted titmouse, Carolina wren, Acadian flycatcher, blue-gray gnatcatcher, pileated woodpecker, hairy woodpecker, red-bellied woodpecker, and eastern wood peewee. Transitioning over to the Green Ridge State Forest later in the morning, we added several more species, including Louisiana waterthrush, eastern towhee, northern cardinal, red-shouldered hawk, chipping sparrow, great-crested flycatcher, and black-capped chickadee.

In total, we conducted 14 different point counts over the course of what proved to be more than a 5-hour exam. Overall, it was a pretty quiet morning for warblers, which are my auditory specialty, but we managed to find a good number of other woodland species, and I was able to identify enough of them to render the test a success. As a result, I now enjoy all the rights and privileges (which are notably few) of being listed as a certified FIDS observer in the state of Maryland.

There is no doubt that passing the FIDS observer test is the most unique and challenging of the bird-related work assignments that I've been tasked with to date. It required extensive pre-test preparation (i.e., paid bird watching conducted at my own pace and leisure) followed by an exciting day roaming around the mountains of western Maryland with an extremely knowledgeable field zoologist. All things considered, it was an awesome field assignment, and I'm really looking forward to doing some paid FIDS surveys in the near future. It's a tough job, but somebody's got to do it!

Speaking of tough jobs that need to be done, no job is more important, more beneficial, or more meaningful than doing the work of God. Each of us has a specific job to do, a unique role to play, in the advancement of God's kingdom on this earth. He is the vine, and we are the branches. If we stay connected to Him and He stays connected to us, then our branches will bear significant kingdom building "fruit" into this world. Apart from Him, we can do nothing that is worth doing (John 15:5). We must remain connected to Jesus in all that we think, in all that we say, and in all that we do such that our lives become an instrument for fulfilling God's divine purposes for humanity. In so doing, we are also fulfilling our ultimate purpose in life, in hopeful anticipation that we will someday hear the words "well done, good and faithful servant". Now that is a job worth doing.

Topping Kenai Fjords

I've had the immense privilege of birding at some pretty spectacular places; places like Ferd's Bog in the Adirondack Mountains of upstate New York, Hawk Mountain atop the Kittatinny Ridge in Pennsylvania, Chincoteague National Wildlife Refuge on the Eastern Shore of Virginia, the Pawnee National Grassland in eastern Colorado, Saguaro National Park in the Sonoran Desert of southern Arizona, and the Creamer's Field Migratory Waterfowl Refuge on the outskirts of Fairbanks in central Alaska, to name just a few.

I've seen Clark's nutcrackers in Yellowstone, western scrub-jays at the Grand Canyon, willow ptarmigan in Denali, bobolinks in the Canaan Valley, black-necked stilts at Bombay Hook, painted buntings at Huntington Beach, and piping plovers at Cape May Point. I've already lived a birder's dream and am just barely 40 years old. Suffice it to say, the word "grateful" doesn't even begin to describe how I feel for having been so blessed in life.

While all of the places I've visited are unique and interesting in their own special way, there is one place that I hold above all the others. Kenai Fjords National Park is the most remarkable place that I've had the opportunity to go birding thus far. Situated along the southern coast of the Kenai Peninsula in southcentral Alaska, Kenai Fjords National Park is a 600,000-acre wonderland of deep glacial fjords, massive tidewater glaciers, precipitous headlands, jagged-rock islands, impenetrable icefields, nunatak mountain peaks, and braided meltwater rivers. It's a landscape that is still locked in the throws of creation as geologic, climatic, and tidal forces continually sculpt and shape it.

Despite the dynamic nature of this evolving landscape, it's a rich ecosystem that supports a tremendous diversity of bird and mammal species. From marbled murrelets to Dall's porpoises, the coastal waters of Kenai Fjords are home to a menagerie of unique species, the likes of which I had never seen before. It's the combination of the glacial landscape and this diversity of pelagic species that makes Kenai Fjords such an awesome birding destination.

Obviously, one needs to charter a boat or reserve a spot on one of the commercial tour vessels that operate out of Seward to venture out into the bays and fjords that characterize this special place. There is a significant amount of land associated with Kenai Fjords National Park, but much of it is buried beneath an enormous icefield. Consequently, the best way to see Kenai Fjords and its spectacular wildlife is by boat, which is precisely how I spent the majority of my one and only day in this national park.

Setting out from the Seward Boat Harbor, we motored due south through Resurrection Bay and out into the turbulent waters of the Harding Gateway. This transition zone between the rugged coastline and the wild Gulf of Alaska is where the sea started to come alive with birdlife. Horned and tufted puffins, two northern Pacific specialty species, became so numerous as to be somewhat mindboggling. This was the first of my Kenai Fjords birding surprises. Based on my pre-trip research, I was expecting (i.e., hoping) to see puffins on this boat ride, but I had no idea that they would be present in such a tremendous volume. Further, I had no idea that they would be so easy to see. At one point during the trip, we had numerous puffins within a few feet of the boat. Needless to say, it was a real treat to see these quintessential Alaskan seabirds in such great quantity and at such a close range.

Also quite common were pigeon guillemots, marbled murrelets, and common murres. These could be found at various locations throughout the fjords, but not in the same voluminous numbers as that of the puffins. With so many different life list species flying, floating, and diving about, it was hard to focus on any one particular bird at a time. Rather, I tried to soak in the entirety of the avifaunal experience in all its glorious splendor. Add in the numerous humpback and killer whales that were spotted coming to the surface amid the raucous cries of black-legged kittiwakes and glaucous-winged gulls, and the show could be described as nothing short of spectacular.

As if the puffins, murres, and kittiwakes weren't enough, there was another Kenai Fjords birding surprise in store for me that day, and it came by way of two different species of auklets. Again, based on my pre-trip research, I knew that parakeet and rhinoceros auklets were a possibility in Kenai Fjords National Park, but I didn't hold much hope for actually seeing them. Miraculously, I got great looks at a single parakeet auklet that was mixed in with some horned puffins and a small flock of rhinoceros auklets at the mouth of Aialik Bay.

These were two phenomenal seabird sightings for a lifetime Pennsylvania Piedmont resident, and I was absolutely ecstatic about it. To this day, I still consider the parakeet and rhinoceros auklets from Kenai Fjords to be the two most unusual and the most unlikely to ever be seen again species on the entirety of my 360+ species life list. They were the proverbial icing on the cake for my Kenai Fjords birding experience.

As a result of my extraordinary day in Kenai Fjords National Park, it currently holds the position of being the top birding destination that I've had the privilege of visiting to date. I have yet to find its equal in my travels across the country. The Sonoran Desert habitat of Saguaro National Park in southern Arizona is pretty fantastic when it comes to birding, as is the Chincoteague National Wildlife Refuge in Virginia and the Bombay Hook National Wildlife Refuge in Delaware, but they are not as impressive, at least in my opinion, as Kenai Fjords.

I hear good things about Monterey Bay in California, the Chiricahua Mountains in Arizona, the Rio Grande Valley in Texas, and the Everglades in Florida, but I have not yet had the opportunity to visit these places and cannot render an opinion. In the interim, I will continue to bird my way around the country, as time and money permit, in hopeful anticipation of someday finding a place that can top Kenai Fjords. I have my doubts, but I'll keep looking just the same.

Despite my skepticism, there's a very good chance that I'll eventually stumble across a better birding spot than Kenai Fjords. It may take a while, but it will inevitably happen. Conversely, one thing that simply cannot be topped is God. Our triune god (i.e., God the Father, God the Son, and God the Holy Spirit) is absolutely perfect; there is no possibility for improvement. God's holy nature, His immense power, His creative wonder, His enduring patience, and His fatherly love are unequaled. In fact, nothing even comes close to God's divine perfection. We don't even have the mental capacity to fully understand God's incomparable awesomeness; He is too great for us to fathom.

Even so, God, in all His glorious splendor, invites us into a covenant relationship with Him. We are invited into His fold, to get to know Him up close and personal. This is precisely what He wants. In fact, this invitation is extended to everyone, but there are a lot of people who don't want or accept it. Personally, given the collective error of our ways, it's always been somewhat of a mystery to me as to why such a profound and incomprehensible god would even want to be involved with us. The fact that He does speaks to His enduring patience and fatherly love, which are far greater than anything we know and cannot be topped.